From Kalamazoo to Timbuktu

A tale of adventure from rural America
to discover the world

Paul Guenette

BookLocker
Saint Petersburg, Florida

Print ISBN: 978-1-64719-696-7
Ebook ISBN: 978-1-64719-697-4

Published by BookLocker.com, Inc., St. Petersburg, Florida.

Printed on acid-free paper.

BookLocker.com, Inc.
2021

Contents

I like to Wave

"Every person in their life should plant a tree, raise a child, and write a book."
– The Talmud

I have an early memory of sitting alone in our front yard on a warm summer day, waiting for cars to pass on Rural Route 1 in Flat Rock, Michigan. I would wave at each vehicle that passed and watch them, hoping they would wave back. Most did. Some didn't.

My epiphany that afternoon at the ripe age of three or four, was that I wouldn't be discouraged if the people in a car didn't wave back. I'd wave just as enthusiastically ten minutes later at the next car that passed. Yes, it took that long. But one refusal didn't change the chances of the next win.

I wondered where the cars were going. That country road was like the ditch next to it holding just a trickle of water. The ditch was silent and dark, appearing still. Then along would come a lone dried oak leaf, floating points up, from the neighbor's farm, going through the culvert under our driveway and on to the neighbor. Determined to go somewhere.

I was small, even for my age, and I thought that the world was so big that there were probably other boys out there named Paul Guenette. In fact, there were probably so many people in the world, that maybe one of those Paul Guenettes looked just like me.

Someday I would act, sing, and dance on stage, direct plays on several continents. Win varsity letters and gold medals, skinny dip by moonlight in the Mediterranean Sea. Climb down into the Grand Canyon to camp in the dead of winter. Live in an African mud hut on the edge of the Sahara Desert, then find the love of my life in Nouakchott, the capital of the Islamic Republic of Mauritania.

While working in Ethiopia, I would fly north back in time to Axum, now an excavation site of the palace of the Queen of Sheba and the Arc of the Covenant. I would climb to the lip of a live volcano in Indonesia, summit Mount Kilimanjaro, Africa's highest peak, circle Mount Kenya in a biplane at dawn, and paddle a canoe gazing up at the Annapurna Range in Nepal.

While living in Barbados, I would learn to scuba dive and to mix a good rum punch, in the Indian Ocean cruise on a dhow with my love by moonlight, and peer at the sea off Alexandria, Egypt trying to see Atlantis. In the horn of Africa, I would drive my family on safari amid galloping giraffes and herds of zebra and gazelle. I would ride a near-wild stallion in the African bush, a camel at the Pyramids in Egypt, and an elephant in northern Thailand.

No dreams as grand as these occurred to me then. They were in my future. I only ever wanted such a grand adventure. I never had enough patience to sit quietly. Maybe I had a touch of ADD. Looking back now, I believe that the seeds of my global adventures were planted in that young boy waving at passing cars from that front yard on a quiet country road. And waving again when the next car came by.

Childhood

"Everybody should keep some grip on childhood, even as a grownup."
– Tim Curry

In rural Flat Rock, Michigan, there was a lot of natural space. Besides our front yard and its fascinating ditch by the road, there was a large vegetable garden on one side, some apple trees on the other, and an even larger backyard and cornfield out back. It was my personal world to explore.

I had two big sisters to keep me in line. They cooked and cleaned, they sewed. They babysat me for free, the neighbors' kids for twenty-five cents an hour – and that included caring for babies, feeding kids, and cleaning the house. We didn't have allowances. But I was a favored son. Breaks were mine by birth. I had a sandbox in the backyard later converted to a strawberry/weed patch. And after dispatching the last of the family's chickens, my dad turned the chicken coop into a playhouse for me with a cool entry and exit ramp.

Our garden gave us tomatoes, onions, radishes, carrots, lettuce, cucumbers, and my favorite, rhubarb. Mom and my sisters canned produce in the fall to store in the cellar and to eat throughout the hard winter. A few times, I joined my parents and sisters to pick a nearby farmer's beans and peas, but while it was real work for the big people, I was just along to stay out of trouble and eat whatever I wanted.

Dad worked shiftwork at the paper mill and Mom was a housewife. It was an emotionally messy household. Mom was a rolling thunderstorm with periodic cloudbursts, probably exacerbated by the isolation. Maybe that's why we moved to the nearby city.

 I grew up in Escanaba ("Esky") Michigan, a relatively large city in the under-populated Upper Peninsula of Michigan. It's easier to be big when you're small like that. This is where I gained two younger brothers to push outside the lines. Mom got a job at J.C. Penney's. My brothers and I walked up 12th Street to Saint Patrick's Grade School. Urban life in small town USA helped the family settle. And it brought me a bit closer to the world.

Esky living was a series of Norman Rockwell paintings. We rode our bikes from my South Side to the North Side of Main Street. Fun, curvy Snake Alley was my shortcut to Ludington Park where we could slide down the summer-burnt grassy hill on flattened cardboard boxes. We built wooden carts from old lawn mower wheels and boards from our dads' garages but never really mastered the rope-and-feet steering. My cart had a bumper sticker that read "Ubangi, Upayee." Crashes were epic.

I collected empty pop bottles from around the high school tennis courts and cashed them in for penny candy at the old folks' Basement Store or at the South Side Market. Mallo Cup coins were valued collectibles found in discarded wrappers. Their trash was my gold. When you mailed in $5 worth, they'd mail you a free 10-pack. That was candy for a season.

I considered myself at least typical if not altogether normal. I was an altar boy, a paper boy, and I sung in the St. Patrick's church choir. I hadn't studied music but I had a good ear. If I sung next to Mark, the other baritone in the choir, I was fine.

People didn't lock their house doors (ever) in Escanaba in the 1960's. One summer day when the family returned from a family picnic, we found one of my glued, painted model airplanes crashed on my bedroom floor. It was a red baron biplane, a favorite. A neighbor girl, Michelle, had wandered in while we were away and she'd liked it too. She tried to make it fly.

Everyone in town seemed to know everyone else. Dad would ask me about a playmate, then sit back and wonder aloud if that was the boy whose dad works the night shift at the paper mill or runs the shoe store downtown. I didn't know.

On Sunday afternoons the family would gather in the living room to watch the Packer game on the black and white television. Sunday nights it was the Ed Sullivan Show. I memorized all of the shows on the three networks.

Our house had an actual dining room, but we ate our meals at the kitchen table. My older sister, Chris, would leave the kitchen with her plate to eat "in solitary" if I whistled too much at dinner. I didn't mind.

In Norman Rockwell's collection, there is a grassy lot for kids to play. Real baseball we played on a vacant lot on the opposite corner of the city block from my house. The earthy pits that our sneakers dug as we rounded the bases became deep sand pockets to define the infield. We wore "play clothes" - holes in the knees of old jeans, and dirty t-shirts for our pick-up games. Whoever was available joined. Toddlers were often enlisted to stand (or sit) in right field.

Years later that grassy corner became a parking lot kitty-corner from Escanaba's hospital. I first saw there my little brother, Fran, when Mom held him up at her second-floor window. Kids weren't allowed in.

In the fall, acorn fights took over. I dreamed of making an acorn-firing machine gun. It would have helped match the neighbor kid's arm. John went on to pitch for a Chicago Cubs farm club. He could sure throw an acorn. I gathered and stored a grocery bag full of acorns in the garage. My dad threw them away when they grew worms.

The garage was Dad's retreat. He'd built himself a workbench and organized his tools there. While he rarely spoke of his WWII service, there was a brass plaque hanging on the wall above his bench that portrayed a German soldier and an American. The German had asked the American to respond to their offer for the Americans to surrender. The American Captain's reply was printed at the bottom of the plaque, "Nuts!" Dad named our dachshund Fritz and told tales of surrendering Germans as the war neared its end, "They were mostly boys and old men by 1945."

In winter, it was all about shoveling snow. Remember, this is the Upper Peninsula of Michigan "way up north in God's country." My dad would get us all out after a snowstorm to open the alley to the garage. He taught us the art of shoveling. Deep snow may need several "blocks" removed to reach the sidewalk. Shovel before anyone walks on the snow. Shovel clean to the edges to make the next shovel job easier. I once nearly died of exhaustion shoveling my neighbor's sidewalk for $1.50. They lived in a corner house with lots of sidewalk and a garage entrance. I was a small child.

Winter mornings were dark and cold in Esky. No bikes then. Getting up and delivering newspapers on foot in the dark was tough. At least once every winter I'd take a spill on icy sidewalks and hurry home with a woolen-covered butt full of ice water. Collecting payments from customers on Saturday was the least fun. Sometimes people hid behind the curtains and pretended they weren't home. But it's how I made those big bucks.

Cars could drive on the winter ice right across Little Bay de Noc to Stonington. Colorful ice-fishing shanties parked out on the frozen bay. Trucks pulled them into place like giant sleds. When spring came, there were always a few shanties that had waited too long to be hauled back and were lost through the thinning ice into the harbor. I imagined the fish enjoying new housing each year.

Spring came with smells, when the melting snow turned grey and then briefly black. Brave flowers popped early. In the alley at the south end of our lot behind the garage the first thaw arrived enough for me to spin my sneaker heel in the dirt to create a "pot" to start the marble season.

The Ludington Park band shell was always good for exploring, and the reeds behind it on the shore of Little Bay de Noc drew little boys. My playmates and I caught frogs in the reeds; we learned the difference between toads and green leapers. We taught ourselves to fish there, catching perch, sunfish, bullheads and the occasional northern pike using worms and bobbers. Once we caught 30 bullheads in a frenzied outing. Mom showed us how to peel their skin off (catfish don't have scales) with pliers and she fried their pink flesh. Tasted like shrimp.

Summer evenings ran long up north. We played kick-the-can or red light-green light in the yards and alleys with a swarm of the neighborhood kids and all went home when the porch lights flickered on – or someone's mom called from their front porch. One friend had a cool attic in their garage from where we could spy on the neighbors' comings and goings. Another had open walls in the basement where we hid our treasures.

Family vacations were rare enough, but usually we would join friends and relatives camping at a clear inland lake with sand beaches. Before I learned to swim, I would just wade and bob deeper into the lake on my tiptoes. Once the drop-off caught up with me and I got a mouthful of water. My big sister Nancy came stroking across the surface of the water to me with a big smile on her face and held me above water. Saved.

The public city beach was just past Ludington Park over a picturesque stone bridge. Though the water was frigid year-round, after three attempts at public swimming lessons I learned to swim. For the first two summers, it was more fun to hide behind the concrete sea wall and play in the warm sand. No one really wanted to swim in the freezing water.

I delivered daily newspapers to make some money. I started with Sunday papers - huge affairs. The Chicago Sunday papers in Escanaba meant that I only had about 2 deliveries per city block. Dad made white-painted wooden sides for my red wagon and I would pull it down the street to make my deliveries. I tried very unsuccessfully once to hitch my wagon to our dachshund, Fritz. That didn't work, though I still smile remembering Fritz trying to pull that heavy wagon up the curb to reach a tree.

When I switched to a morning daily (Milwaukee papers, with about the same rate of two deliveries per city block), the papers were smaller, and I could use my bike with wire baskets on the back. A friendly milkman would slip me a chocolate milk whenever our paths crossed. It was an early morning paper after all.

The First 90:
We rode our bikes all over Escanaba. Someone learned that the guy at the airport was offering airplane rides for $1.50 and 3 playmates and I decided that was a good idea on one day of another endless summer. My dad, however, wouldn't top up my $0.90 so I went along anyway with Rick, Bill, and Dan - just to watch. The airport guy agreed with us over the counter that indeed airplane rides were available for $1.50 a passenger. My three buddies ponied up and I stood back. The pilot said "What about you?"

"I don't have enough money," I replied.

"How much do you have?"

Solemnly I informed him "Ninety cents."

"Well give me that and you can come too," he explained.

That led to our first flight over Escanaba. Bill and I were strapped together into one of the backseats. Rick got to co-pilot. My first magical air flight wound from the airport to the beach, up the coast, out over the bay, and back; we crisscrossed the city for what seemed like ninety minutes. Thanks airport guy for my first "$0.90" flight of so many that eventually led me to 90 countries and flights around the world.

Grade School:
Classes were large at my Catholic grade school, and some of the nuns were very old. The Principal, Sister "B", was nearly blind. I once sailed a paper airplane across the front of the classroom right in front of her while she was at the lectern and she didn't notice – to the delight of my classmates. Attention span again. Pay attention, Paul.

I loved my third-grade teacher, Sister "R," who skipped down the hallway with us, a big smile on her face, twirling the large wooden beaded rosary that she wore. She was flying nun all black and white and joy. Years later, when I was off in Africa in the Peace Corps, my Mom would run into the then quite elderly Sister in a store and her eyes would light up; she'd ask how Paul was doing.

In my open-side sixth-grade desk, I created little machines and launchers using paper clips, ink cartridges, erasers and rubber bands with my hands working out of sight while staring mindlessly at my teacher, Sister "D" posed at her lectern. My buddy John, sitting across the aisle from me, was just as curious but he wasn't so lucky. One of his "launchers" went off by accident and shot a folded paper wad straight into Sister's forehead in front of the class. Hit her right in the wimple! John was always getting into trouble; he may be in prison somewhere today.

When marching single file from school to church outside in the winter, I couldn't resist touching the snow to see if it was "packy." For my "punishment" I (and three equally guilty classmates) had to make a hundred snowballs bare-handed at recess.

Whatever my attention span troubles, the nuns and I discovered together that I was bright. I figured out arithmetic. I won some class spelling bees. They let me teach seventh and eighth-grade math when Sister "B" was out sick.

Scouts:

Boy Scouts offered me the opportunity to sleep away from home, wander in the woods, light fires, and smoke rolled-up leaves with my friends. The Troop Leader sets the tone for whether your scouting experience is rich or drab. Ours was grand. We canoed the boundary waters of northern Minnesota on a ten-day trip, seeing other people only on day one and day ten. We departed out of a canoe base in Northern Minnesota. The guide "packed" our food by standing loaves of white bread on end in a wooden box, then jumping up and down on the cover, turning

Ontario, Ten Cents
I remember most the isolation
Ten days in canoes with only us
And the immense sky
The clear water over which we
paddled, smooth stones under

Or perhaps I remember most the
black bear standing
That surprised me on a portage
Just eating his berries
I backed up silently tracking my
footsteps

I remember too the several moose
Dotting the lakes' edges
And the 36" northern pike Jim caught
from our canoe
This trip tired me of eating fish

The camp sites we chose
Peninsulas under pine fingering into
the lake
Each a painting of forest and water
One where I found the 1909 dime

the loaves into virtual decks of flat white bread playing cards. Easy to backpack. Our deft fingers would unpeel slices from the pack to make lunch-on-the-trail "pb & j" sandwiches.

We saw moose and eagles daily. I saw my first black bear, up close and personal; luckily, he was more interested in eating berries than me. With our grey tin cups, we drank water directly out of clear streams – I could see the rocks on the bottom.

We stopped and camped every night. I found a 1909 dime lying on the rocky ground where some fur trapper had dropped it 50 years earlier. It could have been one of my ancestors. One night I discovered wondrous glowing algae in a forest's rotting stump. But after catching and eating fish twice a day for ten days, this trip put me off fish for the rest of my life.

On another scout trip, we took our canoes straight north 400 miles on a train through Ontario to James Bay. We travelled second class and then posed for photos outside the train with our friendly and tipsy Indian travel companions. Upon arrival in Moosonee, Ontario we portaged our canoes down the main street to the Eagle River, where we lashed together pairs of canoes and paddled across to Moose Factory Island to camp.

Our troop regularly participated in camping "jamborees" competing at knot-tying and first aid with other scouts. We also did winter Klondike derbies. Sleeping in pup tents in the winter is a serious affair that far north. I'm amazed that with my cheap sleeping bag in that nasty weather I didn't freeze to death. We took a bus ride north to the Ice Festival in Houghton-Hancock where I slid down a giant ice slide with popsicles for the taking stuck in the frozen side rails. I achieved a rank of Life Scout with a slew of merit badges, multiple 50-miler awards, and service as Senior Scout Leader. It would have taken more patience, and more serious work than I was willing to do, to become an Eagle

Scout. "Life" was enough for me. Indeed, life was my consistent goal.

High School:

Before running was cool, I became a distance runner, discovering the inherent joy of just running, running by myself unbidden around my block and running laps in my grade school gym after lunch. I developed into a scrawny little kid all legs and lungs. I could run further than anyone else, even in 1966 when I graduated from St. Patrick's Grade School and High School beckoned.

In Holy Name High School I earned varsity letters all four years in x-country and track. As one of only two freshmen to earn varsity letters in the fall, I was an instant big man on campus, though I was still so small that my Mom had to knit me a letter sweater in order to wear my varsity letter. They weren't available in my size! The one that Mom knit for me was barely large enough to hold the HN on my chest.

At one high school track practice, Coach told me to go run laps around the school's practice field. At the end of practice, I was still running, and coach asked me how many laps I'd run. "Forty-two" I told him; that was about seven miles. He asked if I could keep running and I said yes. He said okay, stop. I won a lot of running medals to pin on my high school letter sweater. Maybe I was the Coach's favorite. When I was a sophomore, I graduated to a real store-bought letter sweater in the correct shade of forest green. A few years later, Coach named his new baby Paul; I always wondered about that.

Learning was only slightly tougher at Holy Name High School. But so were the Dominican Nuns and Christian Brothers who taught us. Classes were serious. Teachers ruled with an iron hand over classes of 45-50 students. I would do anything they asked.

One sister was known behind her back to students as "Hank the Tank" because of her size, though her heart was also large. When during her speech class we were tasked with organizing a radio station, my group boldly chose Radio HANK, standing for "Help and Needed Kindness," based on community service and outreach. Hank let it play.

I enjoyed theatre because I liked my English teacher, a Christian Brother who directed our plays. He treated us as young adults. I liked the stage, the lights, the laughs, and the applause. I acted in musicals, dramas and comedies including Aristophanes' *The Birds*, and Mary Rogers' *Once Upon a Mattress*. I learned the soft shoe, the waltz, and tap dance moves.

My favorite role was the Artful Dodger in *Oliver*. He's the streetwise imp that takes Oliver under wing and teaches him the ways of the street gang. It frightened my Mom at one performance when during the pickpocket chase scene, I stepped in front of the classmate playing the pursuing cop, and his elbow sent me flying off the scaffolding in a full backflip splatting onto center stage. Someone seated next to mom whispered, "How can he do that every night?" I didn't! This wouldn't be the last time though, that I scared the hell out of Mom.

College – An Intensely Academic Atmosphere

"Study hard what interests you the most in the most undisciplined, irreverent and original manner possible."
- Richard Feynman

College for me was always assumed to be what followed high school, remarkable since no one else in my extended family had graduated from college yet. Mom and Dad didn't have much money, so I followed up on all scholarship opportunities. I applied and was admitted to Notre Dame, but they didn't offer financial aid to Freshmen. Kalamazoo College did. And they had an overseas study program for juniors that spelled adventure. So off to Kalamazoo I went. My Father-in-law remains disappointed to this day that I didn't attend Notre Dame, even though had I, he wouldn't have met his daughter and he wouldn't have become my Father-in-law.

College was my growing up. I was away for the first time from the watchful eyes of my parents, the Dominican nuns and Christian brothers, yet enrolled in what was described as an intensely academic atmosphere – at a small Baptist liberal arts college in a small Midwestern town. I balanced rock and roll, recreational drugs, and the pursuit of sex with ministers' daughters, while trying my best to cover coursework.

My entrance to the college campus coincided with the arrival of the cross-country team, who became my core group of friends through college and beyond. As a freshman, I became the MVP on the young cross-country team, while also earning the "Puppy" award for most creative complaining. This latter award was simply a case of my "listening to my body," and explaining my ailments with a little flair. The concept of listening to your body rather than running through pain only gained mainstream acceptance in the running world several decades later.

One 10-mile practice run was on the roads of Kalamazoo in the crisp fall air. I began to feel a rubbing irritation we called "crotch burn" so I stopped running and began to walk. Coach came alongside in his car a few moments later and asked me why I was walking.

"My jock is rubbing," I said.

"So, take it off," he responded before driving off. I was in a pretty clear though still urban area, so I dropped my shorts and removed the offending jockstrap before replacing my shorts. That worked for a short while until I was again reduced to walking.

Sure enough, along came Coach Rollo who rolled down his window to ask, "What is it this time?" I answered him that my dick was banging around when I ran and that the tip was getting cold where it hung out below my running shorts. Coach let me walk the rest of that practice run.

Cross-country was a great way to get to know my teammates, and the members of the football team with whom we shared the locker room. Fall's homecoming was a big affair. Somehow, I found myself on the homecoming court! AND coach told us that we also were having a cross-country meet that same day, finishing on the track in front of the cheering football game stands. This was my shot at a rare Freshman moment of glory.

Except nearing the end of the 4-mile run, as I led all runners into the fenced area surrounding the stadium and practice fields, I turned the wrong way. The opposing runner who was running second, of course followed me – it was my home course. Our second runner, then in third place, shouted out to us as he headed away on the correct path. The two of us reversed course and set off in pursuit. We couldn't catch him though, and I ended up finishing third in front of the stands due to my wrong-way finish. We still won the meet.

My first college roommate at the cross-country team's early arrival, Bill, was destined to become an electrical engineer (and eventually Best Man at my wedding). We wanted to explore our extra-sensory perception talents. Bill "found" a flashing yellow light in a nearby street and brought it to our dorm room. We cutout standard shapes (heart, circle, square, diamond) and tested ourselves and random visitors at sending and receiving. We never took notes or tabulated our data, but we drew some conclusions. While many students were totally ineffective, some visitors were significantly better at sending or receiving. Some were both. Bill and I were very good, both transmitting and receiving, especially to and from each other.

One weekend, Bill went home for a family visit, and when he returned to our dorm room on Monday he asked, "Did you get any strange "feelings" on Saturday evening?" I thought for a moment and then replied, "Yeah, lots! We had a party Saturday night." Subject dropped.

But the next evening, just before dropping off to sleep, I asked Bill, "Hey, what did you mean asking about strange feelings on Saturday?"

Now I had Bill's full attention. "I can't prompt you," he said, "just tell me about your evening."

So, I began to recount the evening's events, running through what I could remember. At some point, I said, "Oh yeah, I told them about your dream and the walk into the valley behind your house."

O.M.G. Bill rolled out of his bed like a bolt of lightning. "What time was that?" he asked.

"Well, maybe around eleven o'clock."

In a low, measured voice, Bill said "Okay Paul, at eleven o'clock, I decided that it was my chance to explore that valley behind our house that I had dreamed about. So, I went down the hill into the valley. And when I got there, I decided to try to send you a signal that I was there. I kept saying "Paul, I'm down in that valley I dreamed about... But I couldn't ask you or it would invalidate our experiment."

Just saying, Bill and I were exploring. We searched and marveled. We considered that a core part of our college experience.

"Hoben 12" was a basement lounge in our dorm that the college had converted into a triple. I landed there in the spring with my roommates, one Dave from Alaska, another from New Jersey. While other dorm rooms had built-in beds and desks, our furniture was gloriously movable. We raised one bed and balanced it between a ledge and a dresser top, put tie-dyed sheets over the neon ceiling lights for ambience, and screened off a recessed corner furthest from the door designated as the Opium Den.

Bill brought us a pinball machine from which he had removed the glass top to make repairs and we never put the glass back. It accepted quarters. We always had space for guests. Friends sometimes brought their visitors over if they needed a place to crash. Nine humans once spent the night in that dorm room.

Bill used his Swiss army knife to saw pieces out of a wooden bracket that we attached to the wall of our dorm room, on which we could hang guitars in ready-to-play mode. Soon we had a couple of electric guitars plugged into amplifiers in our *dorm room cum rock studio*. When my guitar strap broke and the head of my guitar split right along a set of keys, the maintenance guys came through with wood glue and a c-clamp. My finishing touch was a paint job christening my electric guitar the "Hoben 12 Special."

Down the hall from our room was a bathroom with multiple sinks. We learned our tie-dye skills there, rudely staining the sinks. New Jersey Dave got us practicing knife-throwing into a wooden dresser. It was fun until we had to refurbish the dresser front when leaving at the end of Freshman year. The maintenance guys helped us out with tools, and we DID refurbish the front of that dresser and avoid fines.

When it came time to declare a major, I was delighted to learn that one could major in Theatre Arts. I tried a bit of everything in the Drama Department, including lighting, set design and costumes (the non-swimmer group). I was fascinated by the phenomena of communications between a performer and an audience, that hard-to-grasp moment of electric delight conveying mood and emotion. Over time I discovered that I did best in musicals and comedies, and that I am a very good director. English became my minor, concentrated in poetry and creative writing. Teaching interested me, so I also studied Education and got a secondary teaching certificate, which necessitated enough Psychology courses to claim Education as a second minor, and Psychology as a third.

I got a make-up kit to use in the theatre and practiced my craft by painting David Bowie Aladdin Sane-inspired lightning bolts across friends' faces on Friday nights. I learned some good tricks and pratfalls. Soon I could juggle, and fake walk into a street sign, complete with noise and falling. A real traffic-stopper that one.

19

Plus, there's the nearly famous "finger toss" so popular with tipsy adults and children under 10.

To play Tiresias, the blind prophet, our make-up crew curled my hair and painted it with white shoe polish. Each evening I glued on my white beard. I drew the line though and declined to put boiled egg "skin" in my eyes as cataracts. I stared unfocused into the lights the entire time.

The Ore Freighter and the Mental Hospital

"Oh the places you'll go."
– Dr. Seuss

Summer jobs back in 1970's were standard money-earning opportunities for college students. I spent a high school summer working on the tourist-draw Mackinac (Pronounced "Mack-i-naw") Island as a busboy/dishwasher at a low-budget restaurant. It was my first working summer at the age of 16, and my parents bought me a Greyhound bus ticket for the 3-hour drive. But it was the wrong ticket. I talked my way onto the correct bus with the wrong ticket and arrived about 3 am, spending the rest of the night sitting on my suitcase near the bus stop until the Island ferries began running at dawn.

That first working summer, I had an Oliver Twist boarding house experience sleeping with three other boys on two bunkbeds in a room with a single lightbulb hanging from the ceiling, a small window showed the alley. The second-story collection of five rooms, had 20 boys sharing one bathroom at the end of the hall. I recall that while sitting on the single toilet, you could look through a hole in the floor onto a table in the greasy spoon restaurant below. It's a view that you don't easily forget.

For after-hours fun, we drank alcohol and explored, sometimes sneaking into the swimming pool at the Grand Hotel late at night. While exploring the wealthy mansion and estate section of the island on a night stroll, I swear that I heard Donovan playing guitar on a balcony and rehearsing his hit-to-be "Season of the Witch." At the beach that summer, I joined, and for a short while I led, the *National Stone Skipping and Kerplunking Contest.*

After my Freshman year at college, my buddy Steve and I went back to the island looking to earn some money. Since now I was an "experienced" busboy, I landed the busboy position at a ritzy

21

restaurant, and Steve got a job there as a dishwasher. We both got free housing in the staff house, guys in the basement, girls upstairs. Excellent living conditions and good people. No Oliver Twist tale here. I was moving up!

Evenings were relaxed after most tourists (referred to as "Fudgies") had left the island. A typical evening was spent on the beach around a campfire, drinking beer and looking out at the lights of the great Mackinac Bridge (Yes, pronounced "Mack-i-naw"). When we saw headlights approaching, it meant that the police were coming – they and the fire department were the only motorized vehicles on the island. So, we'd walk the beer crate a few steps into the water and sit back down by the fire to greet the cops. No arrests were made.

I turned 18 while working there that summer as the Viet Nam war raged and I was anxious to learn my draft lottery number. The draw results were supposedly out and one of our cooks was also trying to learn his possible life-changing status. I politely asked a gentleman in the restaurant with his newspaper to help us out. He asked me for our birthdays. Then he told me that the chef was lottery #4. And that I was #12. These low numbers meant that we would be drafted the following January! I was fortunate, however, to be allowed by the Selective Service to retain my college deferment to continue my education. Those a year younger were not so fortunate, were to be drafted out of college. War sucks.

One of my housemates had a ship reference book to look up the different ore boats travelling the Mackinac Straits as they passed by in the channel. You could look them up by chimney patterns, names, etc. When Steve acquired a 2-man inflatable life raft, he and I decided to take his girlfriend, Kay, on a paddling voyage across the channel from the house, to a lighthouse on the point opposite us. Everything was going swimmingly until we spotted an ore ship on the horizon.

We thought that it was so far away, and we were so close to the island lighthouse, that we had nothing to worry about. Except the ship was moving faster than we thought. And the shipping deep channel as it turns out is very near the island and lighthouse. Pretty soon they were right over us. We could hear crewmen swearing at us in Canadian French from the bow as the ship suddenly turned – toward the island! Yikes. We reversed course away from the island, paddling furiously, while girlfriend Kay (ballast) in the center of the raft began to splash her hands on both sides of the raft while screaming at us "Paddle, you fuckers!"

We were concerned about being sucked into the ship's wake, and ultimately concerned about being picked up and arrested by the Coast Guard. After the ship passed, we hurried onto the island and hid ourselves and the raft in the bushes. Kay swore that Steve and I would have to paddle back alone and retrieve her with a helicopter since there was no way she was going to "raft" back with us. We calmed her and when the coast was waaay clear, we "paddled like fuckers" back to our island paradise.

That's when the ship reference book came into play. Our housemates had watched the drama unfold from the front porch. They informed us that our close-encounter freighter was a 600-foot Canadian iron ore carrier.

I wanted to reach the fabled East Coast of the U.S. and in my sophomore year Kalamazoo College offered a career service opportunity during Spring Quarter. The most exciting job in the catalog responding to my wanderlust was working in a public mental hospital (Please Paul, they are called "residential treatment centers") in New Jersey administering a behavior modification program on the adolescent ward. I claimed a Psychology major in my application and won the position. So off I went to intern at a residential treatment center in Cedar Grove, New Jersey.

The massive red brick complex operated two adolescent wards of about 20 patients each, one for the behavior problem youth, another for the withdrawn and quiet kids. Like all wards they were always locked. I was assigned to the outburst and unruly ward where I got to know the staff and management team, and our young residents. Only once did I do a double shift to fill in for someone on the quiet ward. The heartbreaking atmosphere there made me appreciate my loud and in-your-face ward.

The hospital was a county facility which outside of the adolescent wards was not pretty. The adult wards that I visited on a rare errand were dark and scary, with a few large attendants monitoring the behavior of a few hundred patents. I happily kept to the well-staffed adolescent wards.

It was a rarefied environment that comfortably led to close relationships among the team. I stayed with my fellow college student counselors in an employee dormitory on hospital grounds where I was quickly introduced to cheap beer in cans. I ate some bad institutional food on ward shifts because it was free. On group excursions to the Big Apple, I saw my first NYC's transvestites, drank Singapore Slings, and attended Yankee and Mets' ball games. Classic East Coast!

Over a long weekend, I hitchhiked back to visit friends in Kalamazoo. The hitchhike on the return trip back to New Jersey took longer than expected. Trucks with loaded trailers take a long time to make it over the great divide ridge. I hitchhiked directly back to the mental hospital, just in time for my day shift.

Work was challenging. I was once physically attacked by a troubled kid, until the big guys on duty restrained him and locked him in the ward's padded cell for a shot of Thorazine. His face popped up in the barred window, red and screaming that he was going to kill me when he got out. I was not seriously hurt, but was granted a few days off to rest and be lazy. When I rejoined the team, Jack was more settled. There was no killing. I decided not to major in Psychology.

The "Strange" School

"Don't be late for your life."
- Mary Chapin Carpenter

At Kalamazoo College, my Junior year foreign study experience loomed, and it was evident that I was not a stellar French student; it didn't come easily, if at all. I earned my only "C" in Introductory French, and the prof was being charitable. In a stroke of desperation which turned into good fortune, I chose to do my foreign study for a semester in Aix-en-Provence, France. Aix was the French study center for those with the least French fluency. Other centers called Aix the "party center" which personally I thought showed promise. We referred to ourselves as the "non-swimmer" language group. Going there changed my life's path yet again.

Classes in Aix were mostly in English at *l 'Ecole pour les Etudiants Etrangères* commonly known as the "Strange School." I had a rather sexy middle-aged French teacher who often posed provocatively while sitting on her desk facing the class crossing her nylon-clad legs. She totally knew what she was doing. French classes hurt less.

My academic strategy was to have the whole French nation support me in gaining my graduation requirement of three foreign language courses. Then I could retreat from what I'd learned was the foreign language monster, conceding that I just wasn't one of "those people" who learned foreign languages. Little did I know how wrong I was.

My buddy from K-College, John, landed as my roommate in a French house. We were so fortunate! Madame took all the money that the school paid her for our room and partial board - and spent it on groceries to make us fabulous French dinners five nights a week. Yes, with wine.

John and I rode our bikes all over Aix's curving streets and byways. Only once did we crash, but it was epic. Peddling fast side by side, we were approaching the *Palais de Justice* with a great curving driveway and porch – that I wanted us to take. John said, "Don't come over." I replied, "I'm coming over." I turned left and John didn't. I hit the middle of his back wheel and bent my fork back alongside the pedals when my bike hit the brick wall next to the driveway. Luckily for me I flew cleanly over the wall and landed in the palace garden, unhurt. John held his line for a second before his bike went out from under him and he landed on an elbow in the stone street. His elbow hurt but neither of us was seriously injured. I had to half-carry my bike to the repair shop where I locked it to a rack until the next morning when they were open. The gentleman repeatedly looked at the bike, back and me, at the bike, and back at me.

John and I were from Kalamazoo College, so of course by Fall 1972 we were both pretty good "Ultimate" frisbee players – decades before the sport was created. John and I set ourselves up at opposite ends of a beautiful flowered courtyard surrounded by historic buildings, each of us stepping up a few stone stairs for elevation. Then we began to play "catch" back-and-forth without even needing to move our feet. Catches between our legs or behind the back. A crowd gathered to watch. "Que-ce qui se passe?" (What's happening?) Then, our reply "Frisbee!" A few months later the University bookstore in Aix began selling frisbees.

Cezanne's "Impressionist" paintings made nearby *Mount Saint Victoire* famous. Picasso's estate is in its foothills – where Picasso is reportedly buried. In a standing position. Under his front walkway. Imagine that.

Our landlord had summited this mountain numerous times, doing his ascent on the "black" trail. Madame explained that Monsieur always drank a glassful of garlic to strengthen his heart before such a climb. We took that for an exaggeration until one morning at breakfast, we watched him prepare a 10-ounce drinking glass FULL of chopped garlic, top it up with warm water from the tap, and DRINK IT ALL DOWN before slapping his chest with *machismo*. Years later studies showed that garlic had beneficial effects on circulation. No wonder Madame professed to go through 52 kilos of garlic a year. She had strings of the odiferous vegetable hanging in her garage next to the kitchen. And she used it in everything from soups to sauces to salads. I personally have loved garlic ever since that stay *chez Madame*.

We learned that one could climb Mt. Saint Victoire relatively easily by taking the more public route to the top, so John and I organized a bike ride to see for ourselves. It was a gentle incline up to the base of the mountain, the whole 10-kilometer (6-mile) approach on paved roads, so we were tired but in good shape as we parked our bikes and began the climb on the "easy" footpath.

Less than half-way up, we realized that our one-liter bottle of coke was not enough beverage. But we were close to finishing the climb - and going down would be much easier than climbing up. We figured to get a drink from another generous climber at the summit. The surprise was on us.

Mt. Saint Victoire has a 4th century monastery at the summit with a sweet water well! I can still picture in my mind that empty coke bottle filled with cool, clear water. Speed coasting home was the frosting on that cake, crouched in a racer's profile, only occasionally touching the brakes to control our gentle descent all the way home.

On weekends, Madame gave us <u>back</u> the cash allowance for those weekend dinners under the unarguable logic that she deserved a break on *le weekend* and we did too. She told us to have a good time, take short trips, and explore the area.

A group of us took a ski trip to the not too distant French Alps. A good-skier friend persuaded me to take a lift higher up the mountain to get away from the crowds and the icy slope so that he could teach me "wedge christie" turns. What I discovered was that the crowds avoided the mountain top because the slope there was incredibly steep. Way beyond my comfort level. I swore that should I somehow make it down the mountain, I would never again come up here.

After taking one rough christie turn, I found myself streaking downhill in what was my habitual protective crouch. The problem was that I kept gaining speed. Inevitably, I hit a choppy area and flew out of control, tumbling and rolling to a stop. My "instructor" came schussing over to inquire whether I was hurt. The tumble didn't break me luckily, though both skis came loose and one of them broke cleanly in half.

Rather clumsily (and sullenly) I walked the rest of the way down to civilization. I went back to the rental shop and in my broken French said, "*J'ai loue deux skis; je vous rends trois.*" (I rented two skis and am bringing you back three.) He refused to rent me another pair.

On a different weekend ski trip, we rode home in style with our classmate who'd broken her ankle when she fell while getting onto a disc lift. With a newly dressed cast on her foot, we took an ambulance the several hundred miles ride back south, treated several times on request to the full siren-and-lights treatment. Then we "delivered" her to her French household, where fortunately as we reasoned, her landlord was a medical doctor.

A group of students took a weekend road trip with a friend whose dad had bought a car in Europe that she could use for a while until he could import his "used" vehicle. We visited the *Gorge du Verdun*, the scene of historic bloody World War II battles. I was blown away by the *Point de Mescaline* where leaning over a stone wall, you could see waaaay down to the bottom of the gorge, while facing a strong rising wind that hit you smack in the face. A rush, certainly. Especially when a perfect leaf rose from a pinpoint below on a magic draft to pass right in front of us – and kept going right on up.

I learned about food and wine, how to eat artichokes and avocados, even *escargots*. In Aix-en-Provence, lunch with my buddy John was usually *pain complet* bread and some *boursin aux noix* cheese. Local red wine from a huge cask was readily available into your own bottle. No labels. I could carry four bottles in the large pockets of my green army coat – while riding my bike home. We signed up for a great wine course every Friday afternoon at the local *Department d'Agriculture* that took us through basic tastes, then reds, whites, and sparkling wines. We graduated.

Our adventurous group enjoyed skinny-dipping in the Mediterranean by the light of a full moon. Near Nice on the French Riviera I swam out to a sailboat with a classmate and we raised our thumbs as hitchhikers. A young French couple picked us up for a sailboat ride around the bay.

I spent a night on a Mediterranean beach in the Camargue at *Saintes Maries de la Mer*. It is said that the three saints, Mary Magdalene, Mary Salome, and Mary Jacobe sailed to this area after witnessing the empty tomb of Jesus after his resurrection. The town became a pilgrimage destination for gypsies. Wild white horses run freely on the beach. I camped in a tent with a Frenchman, a German, and three American women. This sounds like the beginning of a joke, forgive me. I first heard Pink Floyd's eerie *Dark Side of the Moon* album playing on a cassette player that night in the cool crowded tent darkness. Very otherworldly.

Pink Floyd it turned out was scheduled to play a concert in Marseilles a few weeks later, a short train ride from Aix. A group of us went there, bought tickets and discovered that they were performing in a classical music hall – with a *ballet troupe*! For an hour, the dancers performed to Pink Floyd's live music. Then the dancers left the stage, the smoke machines kicked in, and the band members slid forward on moving set pieces onto the stage for the second hour of the evening's music, a bit louder. It no longer seemed like an opera house at all.

At the climax of the concert, the stage's classical Greek pillars tipped forward toward the audience, and as the music magically whipped its sound around the perimeter of the hall, flame shot out of the pillar cannons at the audience! Among the three elderly women in front of us, who presumably had come to see the ballet, the woman in the center fell sideways onto her neighbor's shoulder. And her friends didn't notice. We tapped one on the shoulder and explained "*Madame, votre ami a tombe.*" She was fine. We were extraordinary.

After Christmas, we had three months free until we had to be back at K-College. I got a three-month first class Eurail Pass and crisscrossed Western Europe from England to Greece, Sweden to Cyprus. Trains and train stations had first-class waiting rooms available for overnight cover or even to lunch inside out of the rain, while watching the scenery go by.

I was following the book, *Europe on $5 a day*, but doing it for half of that. On arrival in a new city, I would check the bottom of the page for the cheapest stays and then browse them. Usually that meant a 5-story walkup to a private room. One elderly woman asked if I wanted her to put some coal on the room's heater. It was January in Germany for god's sake, so of course I said yes. The next morning when paying for my room, I learned that there was a supplement charge for my coal.

Thank heavens my oldest sister was living in Annemasse, France near Geneva, Switzerland. Every few weeks or so, she would collect me from the train station, feed me and clean me up, then drop me back at the station with some refreshed pocket money.

On one particular train trip east to Italy, a group of us were enjoying our 6-seat first class cabin when we were joined by a young American who was traveling with his parents elsewhere on our car; no dummy, he suggested it would be more fun to ride with us, so we squeezed him in. No sooner had he sat down than he suggested we play strip poker. Though we hadn't yet been visited by the conductor to check our tickets, we nodded our concurrence. And he turned over seven cards, one for each of us. Then he pointed to the low card which had fallen to Diane. As she removed her sweater, we realized that we were all in, because Diane was NOT a girl that we'd have guessed willing to get naked publicly, or even privately. In no time at all, our surprise "visitor" had continued to turn cards over until all seven of us were stark naked.

Then two things happened in rapid sequence. Our new friend began to make out with one of our young ladies (NOT Diane). Then his father came visiting, opened the sliding door and insisted on someone giving him a cigarette.

At this point, I decided to put on some clothes to visit the restroom at the end of our car. On returning to our cabin, I found a group of passengers in the train car's narrow hallway peering through the crack in our curtains. I said, "qu'est-ce qui se passe?" ("What's happening?") And I slid open the door and slipped into the cabin. We all got dressed. Then conductor came by to check tickets. No arrests were made.

Our student group visited as far east as Greece. This required taking an overnight ferry from Patras, Italy. Fortunately, there was a discounted student rate which meant we sat on benches in the hold. But the half-way stop to Greece was the island of Corfu. For no additional cost, we stopped for an overnight at this lovely isle. We rented mobilettes, glorified motorized bikes, to tour. John and

I were learning that 50 kph was our top speed on the bikes when we met several others from our group, riding the opposite direction. We all stopped to reconnoiter. One rider failed to complete her turn-around and suddenly disappeared. When we approached the spot where she had disappeared, we found her standing in a 6-foot deep hole, next to her bike. The bike was standing on its front wheel; luckily, she was standing on her feet. No harm no foul.

On arriving in Patras, Greece, we took a public bus to Athens. At the Athens bus station, we were greeted in broken English by an affable elderly gentleman, the proprietor of Friendly John's, the best place to stay cheaply in Athens. Our bargained rate of a dollar a night per person for the seven guests was just right. And that included a "breakfast" of some bread and a cup of weak tea.

My roomie John's twenty-first birthday fell while we were visiting Athens. Since our group comprised half of the hotel's occupancy, we determined that we could have a birthday party AND invite all hotel guests to the party. Hotel management was not in residence in the evening. As it turned out, Friendly John did show up at our party about 1:00 am to inform us that he had received a noise complaint – from the hotel next door! We quieted and dispersed.

After an eventful short week of visiting the Parthenon, the Acropolis, running a lap on the original Olympic track, meditating on the Oracle at Delphi, and selling a pint of my blood (bought sandals and a bottle of wine), it was time to move on. Friendly John beseeched us to stay another night, asking what would change our minds and stay another night. "Eggs for breakfast," we cried! "Done" replied Friendly John. So, we stayed another night and wondered at the table the next morning how he could possibly serve us eggs without upsetting the other guests. Lo and behold, as we sat down with our coffee and tea, he came discretely out of the adjacent pantry and carefully passed each of us a single, white, hard-boiled egg. Well done, Friendly John, well done.

No Arrests Were Made

"What we learn with pleasure we never forget."
- Alfred Mercier

Senior year at Kalamazoo College meant that it was time for my Senior Independent Project. Since I was getting a teaching certificate, this meant a stint doing student teaching. Traditionally, people went home and taught at their high school, but I wanted to go somewhere new. I moved into my then college roommate's house to teach at his high school in Wooster, Ohio.

For three months that winter I taught at his alma mater, and helped coach the state champion speech and debate team. I lived a little bit of his previous life with his sweet Mom, his rowdy little brother, and his cute sister. When he came home for a visit, we made an incredibly large-breasted snow woman in the front yard that we dubbed *Anitra, Queen of the Harem* after a memorable role that I had played in Ibsen's *Peer Gynt*. (The line I remember delivering from a doorway, pushing my large foam-padded chest up into the star's face, "What do you want?!")

I had my first and only car accident in a white-out snowstorm in Wooster. It was a gentle fender-bender. Nice cop, but I had to appear in court. The cop explained that I was visiting Wooster and that it was snowing hard. The Judge dismissed with no fine. No arrests were made.

In the spring, I drove my cool white 1969 Rambler Rebel hardtop through the flooded areas in Northern Ohio to get back home to Michigan. I only knew one route. After I ignored the flood warning signs, traffic all but disappeared. I was reduced to driving through floodwaters by aiming between fence posts. I made it.

Graduation that spring was great fun until it turned traumatic. Family members were seated on the grassy quadrangle of

Kalamazoo College on a sunny day in early June 1974. We had cap and gowns - the whole shebang. A streaker made an appearance. As the streaker walked solemnly across the stage just behind him, the speaker made a comment about American freedoms, drawing laughter and applause.

But after shaking the College President's hand and returning to my seat, I discovered that my "diploma" was empty but for a brief note. It turns out that even though I had sufficient credits to graduate, the final quarter's Ornithology course had failed me. That failure meant that I was short one required science credit.

I made up the credit in the fall by taking *Physics of the Cosmos* while earning a few bucks directing the play, *Mash,* at a Catholic high school in Kalamazoo. I remember the drama Brother nixing my initial casting of a hot blond to play "Hot Lips." The production went very well, even with a brunette playing Hot Lips. The cast party was at my Kalamazoo "adult" residence off-campus, the group house on Allen Blvd. No arrests were made.

Back home, visiting my folks with buddy Bill, my parents surprised me by suggesting that I have a party to celebrate. She remarked that while growing up I hadn't hosted a single party. It certainly made sense to me. I called my friends and basically informed Esky that the Saturday night party was at my house. Mom made a big pot of chili, we rolled up the rugs to make room for dancing. Then she and my dad went upstairs, their parting line, "Don't worry about noise, we aren't coming back downstairs until tomorrow."

We had a rip-roaring party. Word got out and everyone came, including friends of friends that I didn't know. Loud music, heavy drinking, smoking legal and not, and much wild dancing ensued. No arrests were made.

As things slowed down around 3 am, Bill and I began the Herculean task of cleaning up. After 30 minutes, we had filled several trash bags, discovered several cigarette burns on coffee tables and the hardwood floor, and we had only cleaned half of one room; we were dead on our feet. My mom drifted down the stairs just then. "You guys are exhausted," she said, "Just go to bed." It was hard to argue with her at that point. "There are some burns," I confessed. "Don't worry about it, just go to bed," she replied. We did.

Early Sunday afternoon, Bill and I came downstairs to find the entire house "normal." It was as if there hadn't been a party. Mom and Dad were watching the Packer Game on television. Trashed house transformed.

Diploma in hand, I drove west with a buddy in his Saab to kick off the new year. We stopped at Universities across the U.S. to crash for free. Colorado College hosted us at the English majors' house. We stayed two nights to watch a <u>second</u> hockey game – even rode the student bus with them.

Despite ignoring the "Do Not Proceed Without Chains" signs, we made it through the Colorado Rocky Mountains in winter snow. In Telluride, we crashed in a seasonal hotel closed for the winter. Someone told us about a back door that was left unlocked in the "closed" hotel. After stealing some raw hamburger through the kitchen door of a nearby restaurant, we cooked it over Chuck's camp stove in our stolen hotel room. The hotel kept the temperature near 50 degrees so the water pipes wouldn't burst. We had our sleeping bags on the beds for our courtesy overnight stay, cleaned up and left quietly. No arrests were made.

Chuck and I winter-camped in the snow on the Southern Ridge of the Grand Canyon then hiked down a steep track *Hermit Trail* and camped/hiked along the bottom of the canyon. In the winter, the canyon has a negative snow line – ice and snow for the top half but melted and warmer in the bottom half of the canyon. At one point in the descent, I'd gone first down a narrow slippery path with a sharp turn at the bottom, sliding on my butt, then waited there for Chuck to follow. He decided to do it standing up and quickly began to slide toward me. In a fraction of a second, I decided to plant my back foot and drive my head and shoulders into his stomach. We teetered a bit but didn't fall over the cliff. No lives were lost.

We encountered absolutely no one else as we moved and camped near the river during our 3-night canyon visit. At night we watched stars and satellites.

Our cross-country pilgrimage brought us to our west coast Mecca - California. Chuck didn't want to drive anywhere near to Los Angeles "highway madness" so we cut west to Santa Barbara to visit some young ladies that I had met on foreign study in France. Then we headed north to see my sister living in San Francisco ("Don't call it *Frisco*, Paul") driving historic Highway 1 up the California coast.

We paused for a sunset break on the shoulder of the road where California Highway Patrol checked in on us. Luckily, we tossed our joint under the car just as Mr. Policeman pulled in to greet us and see if everything was alright. No arrests were made.

Later that evening, we picked up a young woman hitchhiking by herself. When she said she was headed to Palo Alto to see Jerry Garcia playing in a bar, we made her very happy by declaring that we would drive her all the way there.

After a great up-close concert, Chuck and I tried our trusty Go-to-the-University approach to find free housing at Stanford University. In the wee hours of the morning, however, only the computer center was open. They were <u>not</u> into hosting a couple of stoned hippies. For the first time in our cross-country trip, we slept the evening in the car. I cursed Stanford University.

Chuck stayed on in California, but I hitch-hiked back east from Berkeley to Kalamazoo, in February, just in time for the Valentine's Day parties at Kalamazoo College.

The Ad Read "Teaching Positions Overseas"

"Man is condemned to be free; because once thrown into the world, he is responsible for everything he does."
– Jean-Paul Sartre

Thank you, Peace Corps. Serendipity led me to you via an anonymous want ad touting "Teaching Positions Overseas." After a long written application and several months, I showed up in Washington DC at a borderline hotel attempting to box above its weight (by using the name *President Hotel*) for a 3-day Peace Corps briefing – en route to Senegal in West Africa in March 1975.

My only worldly possession of any value was my *Hofner* electric six-string guitar. With a violin-shaped body, it resembled Paul McCartney's Beatles' bass. It featured an internal fuzz box powered by a 9-volt battery. I figured that bringing it along was better than leaving it behind despite the risks, so my college best buddy and roommate, Bill, fashioned me a portable battery-powered guitar amplifier and off to Africa I went with electric guitar and amp as my luggage and $10 in my pocket.

Our in-country training was in Senegal's capital city, Dakar. My group of 17 new volunteers were housed in a school dormitory while learning local languages Wolof and Pulaar/Fulani, and the basics of rural development. Our dorm near a cliff overlooked the stony beach of the Atlantic Ocean. A few elderly men were visible sitting on the sand beach breaking rocks with a hammer, turning a pile of rocks into a pile of smaller rocks. It seemed to my naïve self that they were prisoners doing hard labor. The hard labor part was correct. But they were entrepreneurs making gravel to sell.

When we could escape, we skipped class and I learned to body surf in the Atlantic Ocean off the West African coast on a small beach near a big lighthouse. There were some huge dangerous waves. When spotted, we'd shout "Wall of water" to alert everyone to dive under the monster. My buddy Dave lost the skin on his nose in a tumbling wave wash cycle. Today they hold surf contests there; a movie's come out "Dakar – Surf City." And the lighthouse that was just out of town has been enveloped by the growing city.

Three weeks into our training, hence only three weeks after my snowed-out flight leaving my home in Northern Michigan, we underwent a "live-in" experience. Second-year volunteer Frank drove several us out the River Road running east from Saint-Louis just south of the Senegal River. We crouched down in the back of the small pickup to avoid being hit by the swarming locust drifting in the air. Frank dropped each of us off in our village, with the "next" drop-off sitting shotgun next to him. His parting message was "I'll be back in a few days to pick you up."

It was 110 degrees and the Harmattan wind was blowing off the Sahara Desert. I thought I was going to die. I spent my two days sitting in the shade, drinking water. The dry wind prevented any real sweat from accumulating, though simply bending my arm left my skin moist inside the elbow. It was like sitting in a running clothes dryer. On the second day I finally peed. A little. It was bright orange. I was uncertain if I could live here.

Back at the training, we were coached in local languages and culture, plus some remedial French. We were taught the basic tenets of Islam, and the *Griot* culture. *Griots* are traditional oral history all-stars, often playing the *chora,* a stringed instrument to chant tribal or family histories. One told my fortune by tossing and reading cowrie shells. He predicted that one day I would have a good job, buy a house, and have my own vehicle. Looking back from my vantage point in the future, he was three for three.

In West Africa, hospitality is big. Very big. In Senegal it's known as "Taranga." One of their acts of hospitality is to invite friends and visitors for tea. This is not English high tea and crumpets. It's black Chinese tea, commonly branded "Gunpowder."

The tea ceremony is a relaxed process, exchanging greetings and conversation while someone, usually a young man, brews the tea in a small pot over charcoal. The tea is served in small glasses in three rounds; each round the tea grows weaker, and sweeter as sugar chunks are broken off a sugar loaf and added to the pot. It was understood that virgin girls should refrain from taking a first-round cup as it is deemed too strong.

After our ten-week cultural and language (and bodysurfing) training in Dakar, I moved into a mud hut in the Sahara and was adopted by an African village chief for my first program, *Animation Rurale*. I learned to speak enough Pulaar to get into, and out of, trouble in that lovely village of Pété.

Locust, Rats, Scorpions, and the Shits!

"I take my chances, every chance I get."
– Bruce Springsteen, Palomino

I was the first foreigner to ever live in the village. And the only foreigner for at least a 100-kilometer radius. There was no electricity, no running water, no telephones, and no latrines. We were about three kilometers south of the Senegal River and 320 kilometers into the bush along the pot-holed and washed-out two-lane "paved" road that ran pretty much straight east from Saint-Louis on Africa's west coast.

The village chief became my adoptive father and his lovely wife, my mother. They told me that "Paul Guenette" was too hard for people to learn so I was named for my father as is customary, Mamadou Sylae Anne. Forty years later, I continue to use my African name on visits to West Africa.

The *Toucouleur* people (read also *Pulaar* or *Fulani*) were traditionally herdsmen who travelled across the Sahel with their cattle following the rains and pasture. A few hundred years ago they settled in villages to farm while keeping their herds of long-horned white cattle nearby.

My village of Pété was founded in 1861. They farmed a crop of millet in the brief rainy season, and a crop of sorghum on the residual moisture from the shrinking Senegal River after the rainy season. They survived on these cereal crops until the NEXT rainy season, hoping to still have enough left as seed for the subsequent year's crops. The Chinese had introduced some irrigated rice fields near the river. The field work for all three crops was back-breaking manual farming, using crude hoes essentially a metal blade fashioned onto a bent branch.

Did I say it was hot? I'd left my Upper Michigan home in March 1975, my Escanaba flight snowed out. Dad drove me two hours south to Green Bay WI to catch my connecting flight. Now just a few weeks later, I could do little but sit in the shade and drink water. Gradually I learned to live in the oven. The early morning and evening were the coolest moments of my day - and I sweated.

The chief provided a mud hut for me on the family compound and embraced me as one of the Toucouleur tribe. My favorite brother spoke excellent French but was away attending high school most of the time. My hut was in the middle of a three-room structure lined up alongside each other like a motel. I was in the middle room. Grandma was on one side, a collapsed hut on the other. It had a wooden frame and roof, covered with baked-on clay mud. Lying on my back on my straw-tick mattress, I could see the white underbellies of mice and rats that traversed a network above and around me. Opposite my door was a small round window, too high to look out. I had a small table and chair, and a small cupboard for my clothes. Out front I had a porch of woven sticks raised a foot off the ground with a thatch roof that allowed me to sit with visitors out of the direct sun.

My meals were provided by the chief's family. Delicious fresh bread for breakfast, less tasty sorghum paste with some dried river fish stirred in for lunch, and steamed millet for dinner, sometimes with leaves added. I contributed what I could from my Peace Corps allowance - adding an occasional scrawny chicken to the pot or some rare vegetables from the market. I lost weight, dropping from 155 lbs. to a wiry 125 lbs. in the 15 months I lived with these wonderful people.

The villagers were warm and generous; they housed and fed me. They made very few demands. The kids followed me around and loved it when I played my electric guitar. If I was disinclined to play, I explained that my guitar was "asleep" rather than refuse.

Despite the physical challenges, there was so much to observe and learn. I knew that the Peace Corps would be good for me. Here I was. My "job" as a rural development agent was to determine what they needed and to help them achieve it. My best effort was to access the US. Embassy's self-help fund to help finance a classroom construction. The village school had two teachers for two classes of young students but only one small meeting room, necessitating a second group to meet outside in a temporary millet stalk shelter with little protection from the heat or blowing sand. When I asked what the village needed, there was near unanimity. They needed a classroom. The Ambassador's fund covered the cost of cement and iron re-bar while the village paid the mason and provided local materials. A second classroom was built.

I helped on a regional well-digging project, supervising some digging and basic construction nearby. My village of 1,200 souls already had a well. It sat outside the village with sweet water 25 yards down, pulled up in rubber buckets with ropes by hand by the women of the village, dawn to dusk every day. They carried it in metal wash tubs on their heads to their family compounds in the village. Someone would help them take the tub down from their heads, and they'd pour it into the household *canarie.* The round clay containers just slightly "sweated" and in so doing cooled the water a little.

Personal bathing was daily, usually in the evening, using a tea kettle of the valuable liquid and a wash basin in an ingenious method that allowed for full body bathing. The best moment of my day was in the early morning, taking an empty powdered milk can and dipping low to the last of yesterday's water, clean and now slightly cool. With fresh-baked bread from the baker's clay oven and some cool fresh water, breakfast was my favorite meal of the day. It dawned on me at some point that I was very much appreciating my meal - of bread and water!

I tried to organize a community vegetable garden. Enlisting a group of interested farmers, we built a crude fence around a designated plot. But about that time the entire river region of Senegal experienced a rat epidemic of biblical proportion.

The multi-year drought had killed off most wildlife and with the return of the seasonal rains, the basic forms of animals returned before the more advanced predators, leading to a ballooning rat population. The government responded with a program distributing free rat poison. The rats ate it all with no apparent reduction in their population. They ate the planted sorghum and millet seeds out of the ground. Villagers organized themselves into lines and marched through the fields wielding clubs. If at any moment you wanted to see a rat, you had merely to look around; it never failed. We abandoned the vegetable garden.

I bought some mouse traps, then larger rat traps, baiting them with a dab of my peanut butter stash. I was catching and tossing rat corpses, doing my best. One rat though had adopted my mud hut as its own. I'd awaken at night as something lightly ran across my legs. This rat evaded my traps, burrowing daily up through the mud floor. I'd return home in the evening, find the main trap sprung but empty and stuff the hole with rocks.

One night, after stamping rocks back into the rat's hole, I shone my flashlight around the hut only to spot the bugger standing on his haunches under my small table in the corner, looking back at me. My moment of truth.

Realizing my vulnerability, I slipped off my sandals and into my boots. I back-stepped slowly to the door behind me to retrieve the pestle that grandma had been using to pound coarse salt. With this hardwood club, and shining the flashlight into the rat's eyes, I approached and crouched. I swung side-armed and hit him hard. He scrambled to the right, scurrying to escape under my bed. But catching him briefly in the open, I rained blows on him until he stopped crawling.

I sat on my bed for a while, my heart beating wildly, resolved to leave the village, and the Peace Corps, the next morning. But the next day I buried the carcass outside and proudly announced to grandma in our local language that I'd finally killed that bothersome rat. I stayed. Life got easier.

The Old Testament references didn't stop at rats. At the end of the rainy season, the groundwater dried up and drove frogs into the village desperate for water. Every evening and morning I'd find a dozen or so crowded around the moist drip spot beneath my clay water holder and I'd fling them out my back "window." There were scorpion sightings in and near my hut. When that happened, you simply called out and the young boys came with sticks, and shouts of glee until they'd dispatched it. One night I met the insect known as a horse scorpion which resembles a large and fast hairy spider. I'd just come into my hut when this hairy giant ran a quick figure-eight on the back wall, ran out onto the table edge near me, and reared back on its hind legs ready to fight me. Geez. I won that battle too.

There were several plagues of locust to round out the biblical theme. They passed through the village in waves eating everything in sight and decimating the rain-fed millet fields worse than the birds.

I didn't work in the fields. I barely made it to the fields to visit and watch them labor under the hot sun. The most dramatic teaching lesson for me was during Ramadan, the Muslim fasting month, when they still worked all day in the heat without water. People often got sick doing that.

Some families had a flashlight, though kerosene lanterns were more common. In an area devoid of electricity, full moon evenings are like suddenly having streetlights; people circulate in the glow visiting friends. During one full moon cycle, we were surprised by a full moon full eclipse. When I explained to one of the visiting elementary school teachers the mechanics of a lunar eclipse, he replied, "Paul, you and I are the only people in the village who know this." The eclipse caused a minor uproar. Men streamed to the mosque to pray – presumably for the moon to return. Their prayers of course were answered several hours later. And village life moved on.

I learned to poop outside the village behind a bush – and to my glee discovered that dung beetles would remove all evidence within 24 hours. *Voila!* You could use the same bush every day. Dung beetles collect your dung, craft it into small balls, and roll it using their hind legs into their underground nests to feed their young! I found this far superior to any public sewage system that we have in the west and wondered how we could pull off that reverse technology transfer.

My crap was like a NYSE ticker tape reporting my general health. It was usual to have some diarrhea from what health authorities identified as "airborne fecal matter." Our standard health kit included meds for that.

I accepted an invitation to visit a nearby village on foot. They assured me that it was a short walk. Nearly three hours later, we reached the village and after meeting the *Chef du Village,* a tailor, I found myself sitting on an embroidered cloth on the raised platform at the chief's hut. I was very honored. They gave me some water to drink and asked me if I'd like to take a bath to wash off the dust from my walk. I welcomed the chance and found myself in the open-air clay-walled area adjacent to the hut with a pot of fresh water.

About the time I'd stripped naked, I felt the telltale rumbling in my abdomen. I looked over the wall with longing at some distant bushes. Too distant. There was no way I could reach them in time. I had to squat and squirt – in the family's bathing area. I used my modest pot of water to wash my mess out through the drain hole in the wall and returned to the family smiling and thankful, doing my best to appear refreshed. I'm still embarrassed.

They had prepared a wonderful lunch in my honor of chicken and white rice. I was really looking forward to my best meal of the month until they poured across the dish a generous portion of what I believe was rancid palm oil. Bait and switch.

Being the only white man within a hundred-mile radius made me the equivalent of television. I was under constant watch of the village children as their entertainment. For privacy, at night I would retreat inside my hut. I slept on a straw-stuffed mattress that leaked old straw powder. The heat was so intense that sweat constantly trickled down my skin. I learned that the trick was to turn over and go to sleep fast before new trickles began. My mosquito net was too small to stretch onto the mattress edges. Every morning, I'd find a new "rash" where a knee or elbow had brushed against the net and offered a feast to the mosquitoes.

There were two seasons - dry and damp. Around May or June when the rains came, the roof of my hut became saturated. The damp part of the wall where the ceiling crossbeam braced began to worry me. The hut next door had collapsed in just such a manner. I wondered if mine might be next. But mine held.

And the brown, thorny dessert bloomed with green grass and became a prairie with beautiful blue ponds spotting the horizon. It was sudden and magnificent springtime. All the animals had babies. Ponds appeared in depressed areas and birthed frogs. Armies of frogs. Birds appeared where there had been none. The grass grew and the cows gave milk. Milk made the steamed millet into a delicious and nutritious nutty cereal dinner.

I sent my news home via *aerograms* to Mom and Dad. Aerograms were those light blue flimsy paper sheets that folded themselves into thirds as airmail envelope forms. Mail took approximately six weeks to reach home and another six weeks to get the return message, so our correspondence was at best quarterly. I realized later that my amazing stories of adventure featuring intense desert heat, scorpions, rats and amoebic dysentery frightened Mom.

The village elders generously invited me to their front row for holy day prayers at the edge of the village. We discussed that I was Christian but agreed that I could do my own prayers. I brought my prayer mat up front to join the dignitaries. And respectfully read from my novel "Dune" by Frank Herbert. Under the hot sun. On the southern edge of the Sahara Desert.

I read a lot while in the village – you could only spend so many hours a day learning the local language and trying to arrange logistics for health and agriculture programs. Books and reflection became a regular part of my day. I wrote a lot of poetry too – my book was to be called "From Kalamazoo to Timbuktu."

Near the end of my year there, I joined my consort for a mid-service Peace Corps Conference in Dakar for discussions around program focus, leadership methods, health, etc. The one thing we unanimously agreed on was that this experience living in the bush was good for us as individuals. We learned much about ourselves.

I lived and worked in that village for a little over a year. We celebrated holidays and harvests together. I learned about the very basic lines of life. I recalibrated what I considered necessities and pleasures. But I had a yet untested teaching certificate that I had earned at Kalamazoo College. After a year of hard service in the bush, I decided to switch to Teaching English as a Foreign Language (TEFL).

"Teach Your Children Well" - in Senegal?

After my initial year of volunteer Peace Corps service in Senegal as a rural development agent, I maneuvered to get myself reassigned to teach English in Saint-Louis (pronounced "San-Louie"), the old capital city of French West Africa.

I was happy to move to a city and have a concrete apartment with (intermittent) electricity and (usually) running water (cold). It was a penthouse apartment since it was on the top floor of the apartment building and my living and dining areas were separated from my bedroom by an open-air patio. Mark Twain once wrote that the coldest winter he ever had was summer in San Francisco. Mine was here. A cold wind blew on the Saint-Louis bridge crossing the Senegal River on my walk to teach at a *lycée*. My cold-water shower became torture in the winter as the wind blew through my bathroom's broken windowpane.

My assigned high school was an all-girl high school. My students were young and only a few really wanted to learn English, but they were clever, and I was a good teacher, energetic and caring. During Ramadan these young girls 12-13 years old were fasting all day, to the extreme that they carried small tin cans with them so that they could spit rather than swallow their saliva, poor things. One memory burned into my brain is of the young girls who began changing their outfits near the end of English class because they wanted to be ready for gym class which came next. Off came the uniform shirts, on came the gym shirts. Class went on. Eyes up, Mr. Guenette.

My electric *dijoncteur* circuit-breaker box was stolen a few times from the wall outside my locked apartment door but otherwise my life was safe. Life was much more social for me in the city though, than in the village, as there was a group of other American volunteer teachers in town, and a nice group of young, professional Senegalese with which to interact socially.

From my open-to-the-sky patio I could see the Senegal River. The local version of public restrooms consisted of wooden outhouses built out over the river. People would walk out to the outhouses, close the door, and crap directly into the river. Anonymous and hidden. Plop! Sadly, I could also see women downstream washing clothes.

In-country travel was routinely by bush-taxi, in beat up old station wagons picking up and dropping off people as they went along. One trip I made south through the Gambia, to the Casamance, the southern slice of Senegal. Crossing the Gambia River was always the highlight of the trip.

Waiting on the north side, cars lined up single-file and waited for a crossing ferry loading. Traffic coming off the ferry to head back north into Senegal provided a parade of people, some of whom might be friends, but all potentially carried news or excitement to break the boredom of waiting.

This day, the north-bound people were telling us why the delay was unusually long. On the south end landing, a truck had driven off the ferry prematurely right into the water. The ferry landing was slowed therefore, because the ferry had to steam around the truck and land alongside it. The delay should be cleared they told us, by the time we arrived across the river, since a large Caterpillar had arrived to pull the truck out.

When our turn came to cross the river, naturally our eyes were peeled for signs of the truck. And there we found our evidence when the ferry again took a wide tack to reach the landing area. Barely six inches visible above the water, bright yellow with black lettering, we saw "Caterpillar."

Teaching exhausted me though. I felt as though I were constantly performing theatre of the absurd, wrestling to keep their attention and engagement. Fighting to teach them English. So, the next year, I extended my volunteer service beyond the anticipated 2-year period and moved to take a position with the YMCA in the Senegalese capital, Dakar.

Our team there organized urban and rural economic development programs – youth poultry-raising and marketing, and the design, funding and creation of a technical training school for the capital city's high-school dropouts. A small team supported from YMCA headquarters in New York and fully integrating into government plans and local organizations, was supporting social and economic development.

It was a logical progression to begin my Peace Corps tour in a rural village, move to a regional capital teaching, then extend my service as an experienced volunteer and move to the capital city. I kept the tribal identity earned in my village. In Dakar, another door opened. I discovered that there was an international development industry. A person could make a career and a difference working in developing countries. Maybe one day I could too.

Life in Dakar offered its own eye-popping adventures. It was a chance to work with Peace Corps country leadership up close, to welcome new volunteers into the country, and to represent the few extended-service volunteers.

My social network in the commercial sector offered me the chance to hang out with a visiting Aerobatic team after they'd performed a cigarette-promotion air show. One of the pilots in the back seat of the car with me climbed out his window and across the roof of the car, coming back inside through the other back window – while the vehicle was cruising down *la corniche*. I directed the holiday

Christmas Pantomime, a British tradition, that we called *Cinderella in Senegal.*

We had enough softball players in Dakar - Americans, Canadians, and Japanese - to form a small softball league. And some wiseacre organized a West Africa Invitational Softball Tournament (WAIST, pronounced "Waste") for national teams to compete. I was fortunate enough to play in WAIST II in Bamako, Mali on the Senegal team. We stayed with diplomat host families and had simply a great time. And we won the tournament!

The Moroccan Baths

"In Morocco, before you even get to the matter of the sale,
you have to coax the owner to sell."
— Tahir Shah, <u>Travels With Myself</u>

One of my memorable brief trips <u>out</u> of Senegal was to meet some Kalamazoo buddies in Morocco. I hadn't visited Morocco during my college Foreign Study and European travels, but these friends had, describing it as a magical place. A gaggle of us decided to meet there for a brief vacation. It being 1977, international communications were challenging. The group was spread out. I was a desert south of Morocco. Dave was in Berlin, Germany. Others were in Paris, New Jersey, and Michigan. So, by snail mail and several broken phone calls we made the rendezvous point in Casablanca in front of the American Express Office and agreed to meet there on New Year's Day 1978.

A parting message from my American boss in Dakar was the rather ominous, "Don't get arrested." As it turns out, travel for me across the Sahara, even by plane, was more expensive than coming to Casablanca from those other far-flung points. But we all went.

It turned out that the American Express office in Casablanca had closed about a year earlier. The more French-fluent travelers found each other in front of where the American Express office had been. Others found themselves directed to various banks that accepted the American Express card.

Thankfully, we found ourselves and gathered our merry band for an impromptu guitar jam session in a small park nearby. The *gendarmes* chased us out of there fast, so we decided to take the Marrakesh Express bus to Marrakesh – which to this day remains one of my all-time favorite cities!

The Medina is the old part of the city, near a traditional city marketplace. In the winding paths of the Medina, we settled on a small "hotel" that would give us seven beds for seven dollars a night. The two Daves had both been here before and the group leaned on them as our guides to activity. It was winter and we were chilly and damp but constantly revived by the popular glasses of hot, sweet mint tea. And we were introduced to *kef* the tobacco/cannabis mix commonly smoked by many Moroccans. The two Daves taught us how to fill a *sipsi*, the local clay pipe bowl and pass it around the circle, refilling it as necessary.

In between rounds of *kef* and glasses of hot sweet tea, we explored the magical spice-pungent marketplace of snake-charmers, bell-ringing line dancers of men and boys, a circus of colorful fabrics, pounded metal trays and figurines, and leather-wearing water vendors offering spring water in ornate metal cups that they wore bandolier-style.

In our tiny Medina hotel, we were free to play guitar and smoke to our hearts delight, which lulled us into a false sense of safety. One of the Daves had bought some Moroccan hash, which smoked just the same as *kif* in a *sipsi,* if a bit more potent. One evening we were passing the hash-filled *sipsi* in our small circle when a knock at the door revealed two elderly uniformed policemen who entered with traditional greetings.

They went to the middle of the circle and picked up the *sipsi,* asking "What's this?" I tipped the hash chunk ashes into the palm of my hand. Touching them with my other hand, they lost their shape and crumbled. "That could have been anything" I answered in French.

After an awkward moment, Berlin Dave said in his broken French that he smoked a little *kef.* That excited the policeman who left his standing colleague watching us and darted out of the room. Back in an instant with some *kef,* he filled the *sipsi* bowl and passed it to Dave, then refilled it and passed it to the others in the circle. At this point, my Dakar departure cautionary message about not getting arrested was clanging in my high head. But after facilitating a round of smoking, the policemen left our room. We were all stunned (and stoned).

The next day while walking through the hotel hallway, I passed an open door and spotted our two policemen in their room. Exchanging greetings, I asked them about the previous night, and told them that they had frightened us with their uniforms. They explained that they weren't from Marrakesh but were currently assigned to work here, and were guests like us in the hotel. They were just being neighborly!

For relaxation, and to warm up on another chilly winter day, Dave suggested that we take in a traditional Moroccan bath. The Daves, who had both been here before, raved about the public baths. The cheap entrance fee and unlimited hot water sounded wonderful. We were so on for some serious body-soaking hot water. After paying and entering the underground bath, we split into two courses by gender, no surprise. We gents found ourselves in the men's' locker room, stripping down. "Do we leave our underwear on, or off?" someone asked the Daves. "Can't remember" was the answer. The two Daves split on this decision, and the rest of us followed the "with underwear" Dave, figuring that removing them was always a future option.

Entering the bathing zone, we discovered that initially at least there were a half-dozen three-sided showering/bathing stalls, open to the center of the room. Here we found spigots and a bucket. I savored the unlimited hot water, pouring bucket after bucket over my head. I could stay here a long time, I decided, chasing away the winter's chill from my bones. At some point I could hear "no-underwear Dave" squealing something like "No. Get away! Get away!" Evidently, going without underwear was a social bathing signal for a young man to join you in your stall.

Getting a Job from a Stranger's
Living Room Floor

"...and there was a new voice which you slowly recognized as your own, that
kept you company as you strode deeper and deeper into the world."
— Mary Oliver

By the time my Peace Corps tour in Dakar finished, I had spent nearly four years in Senegal (early-1975 to late 1978) and learned to speak French well enough that for the rest of my life, the French would think I'm Canadian. And Canadians think I'm French!

As a kid I learned English as if it's the only language in the world. In high school I had studied Latin for two scary years because it was a *Catholic high school*, duh. Then at Kalamazoo College, three units of a foreign language was obligatory, so I studied French. Equally scary. You had to learn each word, one at a time. And then tenses, cases, possessives, etc. Not fun. Foreign study in Aix-en-Provence helped me limp to the required third unit of a foreign language. At that point I was happy to accept my fate as one of those people to whom languages just don't come easily. Life plays tricks. And communicators got to communicate.

I made some life-long friends in the Peace Corps. I added new circles of friends from the representatives of regionally based businesses. As my Peace Corps service came to its end, I realized that there was an industry that could support my continued international life adventure AND impact change on the world's neediest countries.

Almost by default, I headed back to my parents' house in Escanaba, where they were kind enough to let me move back into a spare room off the garage. Bouncing around back in the U.S. had me itching to go back overseas, but I wasn't sure how to make that happen.

I made a trip downstate to visit my buddy, the other Bill, at his folks' house in St. Joe's. We decided to head to his apartment in Kalamazoo for a fun weekend. While there we went out to a party at yet another friend's house...where late at night someone lent me a pillow and blanket to sleep on the stranger's living room floor.

Too early the next morning the phone rang, someone answered it and called out "Is there a Paul Guenette here?"

A prospective employer had called my home in Escanaba, where they were directed to call Bill's parents in St. Joe, Michigan. Bill's parents told them to call Bill's apartment in Kalamazoo, where Bill then instructed them to call the house where I'd spent the night. They were looking for me – and they were getting tired of hunting. They were obviously a lot more awake than I was at this point.

But the call led to an interview at their offices in Washington D.C. where an important consideration was my speaking French. Before I knew it, I had a job as a project administrator on a rural development project in the Islamic Republic of Mauritania.

The company hired me in January 1979, and I began to receive paychecks every two weeks, but procedural approval delays in Mauritania meant that they weren't yet ready to receive the overseas team. Sweet. I had a new job and with a regular paycheck coming in. I was enjoying my hometown - and I was staying with my folks until I'd be greenlighted to fly back to Africa.

I stocked up on a case of canned soup and another of peanut butter for my sea freight shipment. In March I bought the only new car of my life, a VW Rabbit, shipped it to Nouakchott, Mauritania. And in April I followed it over.

Mauritania is on the Atlantic coast of West Africa just north of Senegal, but it's even more in the Sahara Desert. It is the Islamic

Republic of Mauritania, less formally known then as the land of slaves and clitorectomies.

The street where I lived in Nouakchott was sand. The connecting streets were sand. A short two-lane paved road constituted the downtown main drag. The very fine sand blew into my house at K-112 through window cracks and underneath doors. The beige powder got into your eyes, mouth, nose and ears. A turban, as it turns out, is a really good idea in places like this. There was no functioning traffic light or elevator in the capital city where I lived, or in the entire country for that matter. The city had a few run-down hotels, very few restaurants, and several shady bars catering to foreigners.

The desert itself began just outside of town and stretched eastward for thousands of miles. Visually striking contrasts of deep blue skies, and softly shaded light brown sand dunes impressed us. There were "live" dunes that slowly changed shape and moved, many times onto the single two-lane paved road running due east. The road had several fatal accidents each year – usually at night, when drivers didn't see the sand drift on the road in time and unexpectedly drove into a finger of solid dune. Or drove into a parked truck with no lights. We were careful to not drive at night.

On the southern side of Nouakchott is a huge area known as the *cinquième arrondissement*, an immense tent city, housing tens of thousands of poor souls. Many relied on a single family member working at a salaried position in the city. *Le cinquième* as we called it, made a National Geographic cover and photo spread as a special world capital that was sprawling, sandy, and sad.

I learned the basics of double-entry bookkeeping and accounting on the job from my boss and mentor, creating hardcopy systems to track expenses, and managing local and foreign currency bank accounts. I somehow managed employment records for the project's 200 employees working on agriculture development and range management programs.

On several trips to visit the project site, 600 kms to the southeast, we routinely drank hot water from plastic canteens stained brown by Iodine purification tablets, or from a goatskin strapped to the front of the car. Only once did I drink from a mud puddle. I learned to drive a Land Rover 4-wheel drive through loose desert sand, throwing the steering wheel to the left and right. Using sand ladders when necessary.

On one trip to Selibaby, a friend asked me to please take their horse out for a ride; they had bought a stallion but weren't able to visit frequently enough to exercise the horse. I promised to ride it while in Selibaby. I discovered a large black stallion which had been locked in a small stall for waaaay too long. Using local saddle and bridle, I got aboard. As soon as the pen gate was opened, this horse took off at a full gallop leaving the village. He tried to lose me several times, galloping just under low-hanging branches of a thorn tree, or scrapping near a tree trunk without slowing from full gallop. I grabbed two fistfuls of that stallion's mane and hung on for dear life. Eventually the horse tired and I made it back to the village in one piece, but I never tried that again. Ever.

The beach was just outside of town, a short drive away. And it was empty white sand as far as you could see looking north or south. This is where the Sahara Desert meets the Atlantic Ocean. And Mauritanians didn't feel like hanging out in the sun on the beach, so it was pretty much ours to enjoy. When my boss visited the capital, I drove him down to the beach to show off my sand driving skills. And ran out of gas. With the tide coming in. I left him with the car and set off running for gas. By the time I returned with a jerry can of fuel, he had pushed the car several meters up the sand to avoid the incoming tide. I never ran out of gas again. Ever.

My buddy Bill earned the nickname "Roll-em" when the Land Rover that he was driving on the beach slipped off a crusty sand berm and gently turned onto its side on the sand beach. We passengers rolled slowly too, saved the beer cooler, then righted the Rover and successfully executed our "rescue" mission of the Embassy guy stuck somewhere in the beach dunes.

Arriving at the Nouakchott Airport you must complete a form declaring all your foreign currency in detail, so that they can check you on departure to ensure you only converted to their worthless Ouguiya at official banks. This airport was where I was also "studied" by an officer, whose glance at my face alternated with glances reading my passport. He was holding my passport upside down. Then, walking to my plane I noticed a bunch of small light green papers blowing across the runway – airport copies of those currency forms.

A visit to Senegal, the country to the south, was always eventful. One such weekend trip to the big city was as part of the Mauritania-based softball team when we joined the West Africa Invitational Softball Tournament (WAIST), an annual contest that drew players from nearby countries who played recreational softball and drank beer. These were my people.

As a Peace Corps volunteer in Dakar I had played second base for the Senegal WAIST team in Bamako, Mali wearing traditional *chaia* pants that were made from four yards of fabric and when my legs were spread, they provided an insurance net for wayward ground balls. Senegal won that tournament.

The Mauritanian team that visited Dakar for this tournament had two objectives: win an opening game for honor, then lose to free us up for social time in the big city. Our Philippine players arranged a hearty reception for the team at the Philippine Embassy in Dakar. We did get our opening game win, then lost. A good time was had by all.

Love Found Me in the Sahara Desert

"When you realize you want to spend the rest of your life with somebody, you want the rest of your life to start as soon as possible."
– Film: When Harry Met Sally

Love found me in the Islamic Republic of Mauritania - at Christmastime. Sure, it was a surprise, a most superlative Sahara Desert surprise. There I was, living the next chapter of my adventure and getting paid to support a rural development project. I had a house with a hot shower, a VW, and a houseboy to keep me rested, clean, mobile, and fed. Nouakchott was an outpost city with not too many expatriates, really on the edge of civilization. The diplomatic and official segments of the foreigners usually were either on their first tour (low rank = last choice) or their final (high post differential payments bolster government retirement allowance). I was a contractor and carried a regular passport.

We made our own fun in this desert outpost, playing on the empty beach, organizing softball on the laterite field outside the city, giving and receiving dinner parties. I learned that the most challenging overseas posts generate the strongest communities.

Bill, my good buddy (and ex-Senegal Peace Corps Volunteer), was living nearby. Together, we made life better for everyone, organizing Christmas parties, Thanksgiving parties, regular parties, pick-up softball games, and party outings to the beach. It was challenging but we weren't suffering. Bill and I became unofficial Peace Corps Volunteer "sponsors" opened our houses to visiting volunteers in from the bush. We offered free beer, food, showers and bedrooms. I came to know all the expats living in Nouakchott – and made many Mauritanian friends.

Since I knew virtually all the Americans, at the Ambassador's Christmas Party poolside at the Embassy, I wondered aloud to Bill "Who's that gorgeous blonde in the red dress?" When he replied that he didn't know, I pointed out that "she's standing next to Rosemary Jones, and I'm going to find out." Rosemary introduced me to her daughter, Debbie, an action for which I am forever in her debt.

A few days later, when Debbie asked her parents if the "young people" weren't doing something for New Year's. Deb's mom suggested that Paul would know what was happening. Further, since they didn't have a phone, she drove Deb over to my house to ask me.

Phyllis answered the door, and when Deb asked after me, she replied "Sure, I'll get him. He's in the bedroom." Deb couldn't very well drop and run at this point. I came out & quickly introduced Phyllis as a Peace Corps Volunteer guest at my house WITH HER BOYFRIEND, TOPPER.

And yes, I knew what was going on for New Year's Eve. I'd pick Debbie up at 8:00. Our second party of our first date was dancing under the stars on the rooftop of the USAID Director's house sharing a champagne flute from the open champagne bar.

Deb and I had a whirlwind romance. She was only visiting her parents for the Christmas holiday, right? And then she returned to her job at Georgetown University.

My boss had a business trip to Washington DC in January 1980, so I asked him to contact her "to tell her to quit her job and come back." That I'd buy her a ticket. When she asked him if he thought Paul would mind if she came back, he replied "No, I don't think Paul would mind that." So much for getting mushy.

By March, nonetheless, it became clear to this brave woman that she should quit her job at Georgetown University and move back to Nouakchott, ostensibly to visit her parents some more.

In Nouakchott in May we got engaged to be married, in July, in Georgetown University's romantic Dahlgren Chapel. All the full-blown wedding planning telescoped into two months. We didn't argue over anything – there wasn't time! Invitation choice, fine. Band selection, fine. Deb's mom still had the wedding dress that she and her sister had worn when they got married. Done. A set of bridesmaid dresses from a canceled wedding were available at "Woody's" Department Store. Woody's also had a French wedding photographer for us who had once visited Mauritania himself! A caterer and food were chosen. A friend suggested a good band.

We still needed a priest for the wedding. A family friend and wonderful man, Father John, agreed to do the ceremony, and he also fit the requisite pre-Canaan classes into a visit in his office and another over beer at the Tombs in Georgetown. We put lots of "love" themes into our ceremony script, called our friends and family. Georgetown University where Deb had worked, offered Dahlgren Chapel, the best place in the world to get married. The woman's club usually booked 18 months in advance, had finished renovations early and had an open Saturday.

Before the wedding there was one good opportunity for Debbie to meet the collective Guenettes – the family reunion over the 4th of July weekend. We flew into Escanaba and I had jokingly asked for some "fireworks" to greet my bride-to-be but was disappointed to find only my parents to greet us at the airport. Mom explained that everyone was enjoying themselves at the beach.

I had a bit of a long face until halfway to their house, my uncle pulled out in front of us on the highway and cruised at what could only be described as "parade" speed, with his emergency lights flashing. When we turned into my folks' driveway which wound through the woods a bit, the scene resembled Beirut during the troubles. Smoke and sparks greeted us, my brother and cousin were lighting fireworks on both sides of us, until we pulled into the yard under a "Welcome Debbie" banner stretched over the driveway. My stately grandma was wearing a Press tag on her sunhat. An aunt greeted us with cowboy hats. It was the appropriate Guenette welcome.

The family reunion was held at a rod and gun club. Our extended family reached nearly 200 Guenettes including over a dozen Aunts and Uncles, each of whom seemed to have had five or more children, my cousins. And many cousins were already growing their families. The event was largely a potluck affair and Debbie met very many Guenettes while feasting on an impressive array of Jell-O molds involving canned fruit and swirls of cream. One cousin had a keg of beer in the back of his truck. Another had brought homemade venison sausage.

One highlight at <u>all</u> our family reunions was the boys vs. girls tug of war. Daddy brought the 2-inch manila rope from his trunk and lined up the "boys" on one end, the "girls" on the other. Debbie of course joined in despite her spike heels and positioned herself between two of my girl cousins who could have started on the offensive line for the Green Bay Packers. Daddy shouted Go" and the rope stretched taut. Both teams groaned and refused to give ground. Then the rope snapped, right in the middle, and everyone fell backwards laughing. Debbie slightly twisted her ankle in the crash so I carried her over to the clubhouse and set her on the porch where roughly 200 Guenettes paid homage in waves and begged forgiveness, wishing her a quick recovery.

Two of my aunts, Sisters of St. Joseph, travelled to the reunion from their Motherhouse in Kansas. There was an auction to raise funds for their travel cost involving mostly religious statues and framed images of a smiling Jesus, but mostly I recall the great joy we cousins had, "raising" the limp arm of a drunk uncle to bid on items. One of the sisters was celebrating her golden jubilee for 50 years as a nun, a bride of Christ. Fittingly, dessert at the end of the picnic was a large white wedding cake topped by, of course, a nun in full black and white habit.

We got married and never looked back. Our honeymoon was first in Annapolis, MD and then in Dakar, Senegal - where I picked up my VW and drove us north back to Mauritania. Best thing that ever happened to me, meeting and then marrying the love of my life. Neither of us had even a minute of doubt!

Our newlywed status in this tiny expat community in Nouakchott, Mauritania 1980-1983 meant that our constant public displays of affection became a "thing." Several romances in the expat community happened and led to more marriages in the following couple of years than I'm sure otherwise would have happened in that dusty, hot city by the sea.

In Africa, we learned patience and that where we live is home.

Fran, The Man Without A Country

*"Border security is the most basic and necessary
responsibility of a sovereign nation."*
- Kirstjen Nielsen

My brother Fran was serving as a Peace Corps Volunteer in Cameroon, just a swath of Sub-Saharan Africa away from our home in Nouakchott, Mauritania. It was natural for him to trek to our house over his Christmas vacation from teaching. His letter was sketchy and mine back to him was supportive. Deb and I crossed our fingers and prepared for a Christmas *en famille*.

I had told some friends that my little brother was coming to visit, partly overland by bus, likely with a few cheap flights involved. On Christmas I got a phone call from Fran. He was very disappointed and down. On arrival in Dakar, Senegal – the country just to the south of Mauritania – he'd been told by the Senegalese Customs that he could travel overland the northern border and ferry across the Senegal River to Mauritania where he could obtain his Mauritanian visa.

Believing them, he took a bush taxi for a long day's ride up to Rosso, exited Senegal and got on the north-bound river ferry to Mauritania. Upon arrival, however, Mauritanian Customs told Fran that he needed – and didn't have – a Mauritanian visa. They said he'd have to go back to Dakar to visit the Mauritanian Embassy there to get one.

A determined Fran took the ferry back south across the river, only to be refused entry by the Senegalese Customs. They informed him that he'd only had a single-entry Senegalese visa, and that he'd used it up when departing Senegal. They insisted that the Mauritanian customs needed to issue him a temporary entry visa. They claimed that there was a phone on the Mauritanian side and assured him that he could call the American embassy in Nouakchott from there and take care of the visa; he believed them.

A <u>third</u> ferry trip brought Fran again to the Mauritanian side. Now the Mauritanians accused the Senegalese of malfeasance, insisting that they should not have let Fran depart Senegal without a Mauritanian visa! Fran would NOT be admitted here without one. There was, of course, no phone. He had no choice but to get back on the ferry.

His <u>fourth</u> ferry trip across the border river brought Fran to Senegalese Customs for a third visit. Fran noticed that it was easy enough to get to the bush taxi station without actually going to the customs shop, and briefly considered entering the country illegally. Somehow that didn't feel like a good idea.

Fran realized that this time he needed to compose the perfect sentence to approach the Senegalese Customs. It was this: "*Les douaniers mauritaniens m'ont dit que, selon mon passeport, je n'ai jamais même été en Mauritanie! Puisque je viens de Dakar, il faut que je rentre à Dakar pour régler la situation.*" (The Mauritanian border guards told me that, according to my passport, I've never even BEEN to Mauritanian soil. Since I'm coming from Dakar, I must go back to Dakar to fix this situation.) There was a pause, and they conceded the visa error this time, allowing Fran back into Senegal to bush taxi back to Dakar, where he found a hotel and spent his Christmas Eve alone.

Senegal was just enough of a Muslim country that the post office, the only place with a public phone, was still open on Christmas Day. He managed to call and tell me of his border "experience". I advised him of a friend and diplomat named Art who lived across the street from the U.S. Embassy in Dakar who might assist him. Now I had an amazing Christmas story to tell my friends about West Africa Wins Again (WAWA) – sure that Fran would miss Christmas with us.

The Mauritanian Embassy said they required a letter from the American embassy, which was closed on Christmas Day. Fortunately, the marine guarding the embassy sent Fran's request to someone who happened to be in the embassy, who said, "They want a letter from us? What should it say?" Fran answered, "Say that YOU saw ME today. Put some official stamps on it. They love those." And he went to find Art.

It turns out that our friend Art was VERY helpful to Fran. Art brought Fran (and his letter) to the Mauritanian Embassy and demanded that they issue him a visa on the spot. Then he drove Fran to the airport, whisked him through customs, and insisted that Air Mauritania honor Fran's Air Afrique ticket and put him on that afternoon's flight north to Nouakchott.

When Fran arrived in the airport and passed through customs, taxi drivers began vying aggressively for his fare. "I'll take you for $20!" "I'll take you for $10!" "I'll take you for FREE!" Then, a polite, motherly woman, a friend of mine, said the sweetest words a travel-weary Peace Corps volunteer could ever hope to hear in that situation *"Pardon, est-ce que vous êtes le frère de Paul Guenette?"* (Excuse me, are you Paul Guenette's brother?) Choosing between aggressive taxi-drivers and a polite woman who knew his brother (We look a lot alike.) was easy.

And THAT is how, on Christmas Day, my brother Fran appeared on our doorstep in Nouakchott, Mauritania. It's having brothers and friends that makes the holidays joyful.

The Greatest Vacation Ever

"Travel brings power and love back into your life."
– Rumi

We left Nouakchott, Mauritania after a four-year tour, departing for good in the spring of 1983. We initially sorted our household into keep, sell and give-away, then in a complicated series of steps sorted the "keep" into weight-specific groupings for sea and air shipments back to the states, and luggage to carry on our greatest vacation ever. We said goodbye to our trusty VW Rabbit for its shipment home. With rounds of goodbye parties we said goodbye to our bar inventory. We left the good friends that we'd made in this beautiful dessert home on the edge of Western civilization. We set off on our multi-month travel holiday through Europe and Asia before returning stateside.

Our first flight took us to the Canary Islands – a beautiful vacation spot just a hop north from Mauritania en route to Europe. Our stop proved troublesome to Deb who was again trying to quit smoking – she was angry with the world for making her stop smoking.

We next landed briefly in Rome, chilly enough in February that we bought ourselves winter coats – and a gift bottle of Amaretto for Deb's parents who were now on their second diplomatic tour in Pakistan. This was their final tour overseas with State Department. The customs officer in Pakistan confiscated our Amaretto at the airport and gave us a receipt to collect it as we departed the country. Tricky that, since we were leaving from a different airport. It's still sitting, presumably unclaimed, in Pakistani airport storage somewhere... sure it is.

It was wonderful to see my in-laws in Islamabad, in a country where they had previously served, and whose culture they loved. Debbie was familiar with Pakistan too from her Junior High School days there. (Check out THOSE yearbooks if you get a chance.) A side trip to their previous Pakistan posting in the city of Lahore included a superb train trip that included afternoon high tea with cucumber sandwiches on white bread with the crust cut off.

They also took us up into the mountains above Islamabad/ Rawalpindi to Murray, where we overnighted in the snow at the Ambassadors off-season residence. Deb and I had t-shirts made which bore each other's faces. This Pakistani entrepreneur extolled us with the beauties of the American economy where an immigrant could run a 7-11 store, avoid taxes, then invest his gains in a t-shirt store back in his home village. Ah, the joys of an open economy.

Departing Pakistan for India, we took advantage of my in-laws State Department link to book our room in the American Travel Quarters adjacent to the U.S. Embassy in New Delhi. I recall appreciating the access to American beer and hotdogs almost as much as the amazing city tour, the Red Fort, and tuk-tuk rides in furious traffic.

We booked an overnight tour to Agra to visually feast on the Taj Mahal, a magical testament to love, whose architecture and style boggle the mind. On the return drive to Delhi we stopped in Fatipur Sikri, a small city abandoned in the 4th century for unknown reasons and still strangely completely intact.

The best stage of the vacation, however, lay ahead, in Nepal. Our arrival there was eased by bumping into someone that we knew on the Delhi-Katmandu flight, an Embassy friend from Nouakchott who was now Deputy Chief of Mission in Nepal. His car brought us to our Katmandu hotel, the Russian Guesthouse, from where we could explore the magical city. We enjoyed hospitality from a lively international crowd not so different from Nouakchott, the most memorable of which was a resident dentist! They knew how to party in Katmandu.

In the spring of 1983, Katmandu was peaceful, beautiful, and strikingly unspoiled by tourism. We walked the entire downtown area in a day, noting a steakhouse that featured a sizzler platter full breakfast for about a dollar. The most intriguing street was named Freak Street. Supposedly a hangover from the hippy days, this was the place where I was repeatedly approached by people offering to sell me hashish. No one asked Debbie if SHE wanted to buy some hash until she bought a purple velvet vest with a dragon on the back. Gender equity prevailed after that.

Katmandu is in a large valley away from the Himalayas, so we booked a domestic flight on Air Nepal to bring us to Pokhara, at the foot of the Annapurna Range. This is trekking country. The flight itself was memorable. We were on a tiny aircraft, sitting in seats best described as lawn chairs bolted to the floor of the plane. I remember being able to see out of the windows on both sides of the plane that was buffeted and bobbing like a leaf in the wind. Out our side window on the left, we could see a pattern of tiny cultivated fields laid out like a giant quilt far below. Looking out the right, however, was shocking as way too close to the tip of the wing we saw a sheer wall of rock flashing by.

Thankfully, a short while later the plane landed on a grass air strip in Pokhara. Our guidebook only listed one hotel so that was to be our overnight destination. With no vehicles in Pokhara however, we were approached on the grass landing strip by a polite young man touting his own hotel. After a dialogue, he agreed to show us to our desired hotel if we didn't find his place satisfactory. His place was acceptable. I noticed pot plants growing in the lobby, but the room looked fine, and it was a very short walk to the man-made reservoir/lake that reflected the Annapurna range of the Himalayas, wrapped in cloud as they usually are. But you could feel the gigantic force of mountains rising steeply from the land.

As we walked around the village, we noticed a sign for a cultural show in the evening at the "big" hotel, so we popped in and bought our tickets. They told us to return at 7pm for the show. We visited the lakeside where I found someone who agreed to rent me their canoe the next morning for a sunrise paddle, then returned for the show at 7pm. They served us a cold beer in the lobby, then led us around the back, to our chairs in the center of the front row. We were the only paying guests! Surrounded by cast members and extended families of the entertainers, we took in the music and dance show, applauding regularly and loudly to express our appreciation. If it weren't for us, there would have been no show at all that night.

Our night in the no-star hotel was interrupted by the violent coughing of someone in the next room who soon after likely died of consumption. But at dawn the next morning, we walked together through the quiet streets, to gentle greetings of "Namaste" from the Nepalese preparing breakfast in their attached open kitchen areas. All was welcoming and magical.

The canoe was waiting for us as planned. I sat Debbie in the bow and paddled us away from shore where we drifted for a while, gaping up at the Annapurna Range of the Himalaya Mountains that seemed to fill half the sky. Fishtail Peak shown clear in the blue sky, white snow whipping off the sharp flat peak. This was the first morning that the range had dawned cloudless in two weeks. And it was all ours. Alone on the lake in a canoe at sunrise, peering up at the massive mountain range. This moment, we agreed, had to be the climax of this amazing two-month vacation.

On our return westward, our first stop was Greece. where we stayed in a central commercial hotel until we found the city's historic *plaka* and its evening street life and moved there. As it turns out, we chose the exact small and cozy hotel cradled just below the Parthenon that my parents and sister had stayed in during their visit to Athens a few years earlier. We took a daytrip visit on a ferry to three gorgeous Greek islands, floating drops of white in the Aegean blue. In and near Athens, we visited all the standard historic sites, Temple of Zeus, the Oracle at Delphi, the Parthenon. I even had the chance to run a lap on the original Olympic track up in the hills. I've enjoyed souvlaki ever since that visit to Greece. On the Sunday morning of our Athens bus tour, unbeknownst to us, Greek clocks lost an hour. After some minor confusion we made the next tour!

Still moving westward, it was on to Spain where a roast suckling pig feast put me off pork for at least a year. I still have the amazing knife Deb bought me as a souvenir in Toledo.

The U.S. portion of the most-of-world tour included a visit first to Deb's family in Washington D.C. where we recouped the car, then drove to visit my family in Michigan where we could most easily convert the license plates from Mauritania's Arabic script to more traditional U.S. plates. That drive on 70-West from Washington DC to Michigan included multiple instances of other drivers approaching us from behind, close enough to see the license plate in Arabic script, then pulling alongside and matching our speed to peer at us in curiosity. Who was this dark guy with a black moustache driving a pretty blonde?

When we got to Escanaba, Michigan, changing the plates was easy. I got the car serviced at the VW place. When we came to pick up the car, the whole garage team came out to ask, "Where the hell have you <u>had</u> this car?" They had removed the dash cover to access the fuse box and found piles of fine, white sand. We had shipped back a few pounds of the Sahara inside our car.

Then we drove across the rest of the U.S. to Stanford, California for our next chapter.

Yes, the Stanford MBA

"You will either step forward into growth, or you will step backward into safety."
- Abraham Maslow

When I decided to pursue an MBA, we shopped around. I say "we" because this was a joint decision with Debbie. We first visited a big name business school on the East Coast, and despite an "in" (The kitchen chef of the University President was a friend of ours from Nouakchott), we found it very formal and non-receptive. At the Admissions Office we were coldly informed that this business school did not <u>give</u> informational interviews, nor guided visits of the school. We decided not to apply since even if I were admitted I wouldn't attend.

Then we checked out the business schools in the Chicago area. One was pretty finance-oriented (a turnoff for me), but another had an attractive semester abroad in a Paris-based business school. We determined that a school in my home state of Michigan would be my fallback MBA program. But since we had checked out the East Coast and the Midwest, we felt like we should also check out that famous business school on the West Coast.

The runaway winner was Stanford. The sun was shining when we visited Palo Alto. People were walking and riding bikes around campus, smiling, and dressed for summer. And the Business School was extremely receptive, the Director of Admissions willing to talk with a prospective student. This was the place for me to study, for us to live.

Acceptance letters came in from the first three applications. And then Stanford's Admissions Director <u>called me</u> on a Sunday morning with their good news.

For the first time in my life I would attend a school for reasons of my own, rather than simply because it was expected. I would pay the fees out of the savings that we'd built up living in Mauritania, and graduate without debt. My MBA was an investment.

We loved the campus from the first. We snagged a one-bedroom apartment in a married housing high rise during the summer before courses began. Residency, however, required taking at least a summer course, so I signed up for a math refresher. I bought a bike. We made some good friends fast. Where we live is home.

New student orientation included a bus trip north into Napa Valley's wine country, and a fun scavenger hunt in historic San Francisco – culminating in Irish coffee near the wharf. It turns out that, similarly to the Peace Corps, fast friends are made in cauldrons, be they Saharan or academic.

The fall of 1983 brought the beginning of first year, the drinking from the quantitative study firehose. The Stanford Graduate School of Business (GSB) runs on the quarter system. First year meant five quantitative courses in each of three quarters, or fifteen core courses, heavily quantitative, to lay the MBA base. I never had time to refresh or look back, it was a constant prioritizing challenge. Focus on the most urgent. Determine quickly what I had to know for a series of five four-hour final exams that would determine half of my grades! Lots of pressure, yes, but I most remember the people, the friends we made, many of whom became life-long friends.

Second year was waaaay more relaxed, although that's relative. It was as though we had passed through the cauldron of first year. The year was three quarters again, but this time only four courses each instead of five. And we could choose some electives. I took Business French and a basic drawing class! There was more group work. The year was more social. I directed the McKinsey

Skit, and ran the infamous Hercules Horseshoe Club with my buddy Jim. Second year was still exhausting - but much more fun.

I fondly remember in one "touchy-feely" class (Interpersonal Dynamics) that gave us the deep breathing exercise and mantra. In fully through the nose with the thought of "Haam" meaning "I am." Hold it deep for a second, then breathe out through the mouth with "Saa" meaning "this." I relaxed all my parts in sequence exactly as instructed - and absolutely went to sleep on the floor surrounded by my classmates! I still use that relaxation technique.

In the fall, Deb and I had season tickets for Stanford football games. In the spring, I often "studied" on the grass near third base at Stanford's sunken diamond baseball field.

Deb and I made a trip into the "city" for the afternoon premiere showing of the much-touted "E.T." After buying our tickets, we found ourselves stretched around the corner in a long queue. And we hadn't eaten. I dashed across the street to a pizza joint to get two slices, but they only sold full pizzas. They promised it in 3 minutes. I ran back with our hot pizza, arriving just as the line began to move – fast. Opening the box, we were walking! I offered slices for free to those nearby. No takers.

Now the line turned the corner to the movie entrance. I tore the cover off the box, folded the pizza and box bottom in half on itself, and fit it down the front of my pants, sucking my stomach in and pulling my shirt over to hide it. I felt some warm pizza grease leaking into my nether parts. They took our tickets at the door and we were in! Once seated, I pulled the hot pizza back into the real world, opening it and rearranging the ingredients across the top of the pizza. Unfortunately, the row in front of our seats was filled with Kindergarteners on an "E.T." outing. As their handlers offered them popcorn, I heard several cry out "We want pizza!" The lights went mercifully down, and the movie began. The pizza and the movie were both great.

We had to choose an academic area of concentration. I chose Economics, more by default really, since I didn't really like Finance, and I <u>really</u> didn't like Accounting. My friends called me the "Econ King." I worked my way through the requirements for the Public Management Certificate and counted my credits to ensure an on-time diploma delivery this go-round.

I was exploring post-MBA career options, and so I signed up to take the Foreign Service Exam - a rich experience. Questions were a bit eclectic. I recall listing some famous building designer architects and naming three international terrorist groups. The experience was in line with test guides that suggested the only way to prepare for the exam was to read the past three years of TIME magazine. And I passed!

The next step in the process was to take the Oral Exam; it had a reputation of its own as being awkward and challenging. The exams were after all a winnowing process to identify the best candidates. Since I was at Stanford, I was assigned to take the oral exam at the Naval Base on nearby Treasure Island. The test group wasn't very large, maybe 40 or so. Four "observers" with notebooks were stationed in the four corners of the room. We played different characters in a sort of "Day in the Life of State Department" scenario – there was a missing U.S. citizen, and we were drawing from a glorified and messy inbox with news bits on local government red tape, mixed security notes of violence, and a reported arrest. The trick was to make sense of it. Passed it.

Deb and I were working on getting pregnant about this time. We were waiting for the news from the pregnancy test (Remember, this was 1985). I got the "positive" news while home alone in the apartment. Debbie was still at work. I made up a bunch of "Yes!" signs and taped them to the building front door outside, onto and inside both elevators, and onto our apartment door. She had a big smile on her face by the time we fell into each other's arms at the front door of our apartment. We were going to have a baby!

We would graduate in June with the prized Stanford MBA (Yes, the diploma this time was inside that little black folder!) at a ceremony in historic Frost Amphitheatre. We loaded up our trusty VW Rabbit and drove back east to begin a new job, live in a new residence, in a new city, and with Debbie pregnant!

I Dreamed of Asia

"Whereas the business community in the West is a community of companies, the business community in Asia is a community of people. In the West, companies tend to do business with one another. In Asia, the deals are all done between personalities."
— Michael Backman, Big in Asia: 25 Strategies for Business Success

That summer, I started a new job working for an international development consulting firm based in Washington D.C. My goal was to learn the headquarters, and the state-side version of the international development industry that I'd gotten a glimpse of in West Africa. Having spent eight years in Africa <u>before</u> business school, I wanted now to learn how folks stateside ran the business end of those field programs.

It was a great season of change for Debbie and me. I was starting a new job after two intense years at graduate school. We moved to Bethesda, MD and rented a house. Debbie was pregnant with our first child. We had new neighbors and friends. *Beaucoup* change! But where we live is home.

I was the firm's first middle-manager. The President and Vice President hired me to organize a support system for overseas projects. When I asked them what I might do to make them delighted that they'd hired me, the President replied, "Answer the damn telexes!" They had numerous complaints about overseas team leaders asking them for printer paper and too many trivial support needs. So, I stood up the Office of Overseas Project Support (OOPS) to <u>eliminate</u> managers saying "Oops!" in reference to a blunder in support to overseas projects.

While doing this, I began to build my resume on short-term consulting assignments. Three or four weeks at a pop. I did work trips to Pakistan and Lesotho, Zambia and Haiti. I was doing economic studies, sector assessments, agribusiness inventories, project start-ups or close-outs, etc. I learned how to operate in unusual environments, become self-sufficient, and how to accomplish technical jobs as part of a team. Each assignment opened for me another project team, another country and culture, another region of the developing world.

One assignment brought me to an enterprise development project in Java, Indonesia. There soon after came an opportunity to join the resident team based in the city of Semarang as Business Advisor. So, Debbie and I moved to a new life on the other side of the world for a two-year assignment in Central Java. Jeremy was just a baby – the twelve-hour time change put him absolutely upside down, or rather downside up, for a few months.

It was a modest expatriate team of three, and we were really the only resident Americans in Semarang, so we worked and socialized together. The house that they had found for me had seven bedrooms and four bathrooms, a circular driveway out front and several front doors. Lest I boast too much, remember that it was a hot, tropical climate and the house wasn't air-conditioned. We had a wall A-C unit in several bedrooms though which saved the day (and nights). High ceilings, tiled floors, and well-placed ceiling fans made the rest of the house really work for us. So did a few house servants, wonderful people who took care of laundry, followed Jeremy around to clean up behind him - the best toilet training it turns out is to not wear diapers inside. Boys do like to aim their pee. And these lovely people cooked and cleaned for us.

Brackish water shrimp farming was great for smallholder fishermen. A nearby processing plant would buy all the Tiger Prawns they could produce and then export them to supermarkets across the world. But getting the 2-day old shrimp post-larvae to "seed" their ponds was a challenge. So, we supported an indigenous NGO to build an open-facility shrimp hatchery to train other hatcheries in the tricky science. It was fascinating to watch fishermen visit the hatchery and buy a plastic bag of water – only to notice on closer inspection the tiny hair-like bits floating in the water, looking like eyelashes cut into four or five pieces. They dumped the bag into their walled ponds and then fed the pond until they harvested large tiger prawns.

Another industry that we supported was rattan and wood furniture export. There was a pocket of amazing wood carvers in the south near Solo, who produced top-notch bureaus, desks and cupboards from the nearby mahogany and teak forests. And Indonesia produced most of the world's raw rattan but was only beginning to realize the benefits of adding value and making exportable rattan baskets and furniture. With the help of several Philippine craftsmen, we strengthened Indonesia's ability to make and export world class rattan furniture. Some products combined the beautiful local cloth with a rattan frame to make things. I still have and use some rattan chairs that I bought there in 1986.

My work required near monthly trips to the big city of Jakarta to check with the USAID client re: approvals, etc. This was an opportunity for Deb and me to bring Jeremy along to the "big city" where we could find goodies like pancake syrup and hot dogs at the Embassy commissary to bring back with us. It also meant that we could revisit our favorite hotel, the Borobudur, where we had first landed upon arrival in Indonesia. Going back was always a pleasure – a bit of luxury, some fine dining out, and maybe a visit with some big city friends.

I learned to golf in Indonesia. Our city was home to two golf courses, one in the city and another grand course cut out of the coffee plantations in the hills surrounding the city. Caddies taught me to play, using an old bag of clubs that I bought there. Every time we golfed we would encounter a poisonous snake. We were smart enough to let the caddies search for balls in the rough. They knew what they were doing moving leaves around. If they said it was okay, we could approach and look at the non-poisonous snake. If they yelped and ran back onto the fairway, we ran with them and took a free drop.

The "real" Borobudur is near the city of Yogyakarta in Central Java, also a magical city to visit. The world's biggest Buddhist monument, the Borobudur Temple, dates to the 9th century. It's considered to be one of the world's seven wonders. We visited as often as we could; my work often brought me to Yogyakarta.

But perhaps the most magical place that we found in Indonesia is the island of Bali. We lived in Java, one of the world's most densely populated islands, so there was an incredible sense of relief to leave the crowded environment and an even more heavenly sensation when we arrived in Bali. Peaceful and verdant, with religious influence from Indonesia's Hindu minority. Our memories are of peaceful sand beaches with palm trees and friendly people. We tried to take all our international visitors there to share a little bit of Bali.

All of our dozen or so family visits to Bali were magical. One of my favorite memories is of Jeremy toddling between two beautiful, completely dressed Bali dancers, holding their hands, happy as can be. The dancers had performed a graceful program accompanied by live gamelan music, the predominantly percussive music of Java and Bali. Another is of Jeremy crouched in mere inches of warm Java Sea but about 100 yards from shore

With Jeremy just a baby, Deb and I didn't feel brave enough to try out the primitive wooden cutout canoe explorations into Borneo, which Indonesians call Kalimantan. But the island of Java had plenty of adventures for us.

I set out to climb Mount Bromo, one of the island's live volcanoes. I joined a small group pre-dawn riding on horses up to and over the outer rim of an ancient collapsed volcano, then across a barren flat lunar-like landscape all gray and stinky, to the newer rim. There we climbed on foot to the live rim, getting close enough to be covered in floating ash and feeling my eyes burn from escaping acidic gases. I was dirty and smelly when I returned to

the hotel but satisfied that I'd seen and smelled a live volcano up close.

A year later, on a flight from Semarang to Bali with Deb's parents, our pilot took a loop away from the planned flight path and flew us around the crest of that live volcano, Mount Bromo, so that passengers could take photographs. I remember my father-in-law joyfully taking snapshots from the cockpit. It was 1987, after all, and we were still years away from September 11, 2001 when the world of flying changed.

The *Hash House Harriers* are often called a running club that drinks. Sometimes they're called a drinking club that runs. The members of the "HHH" are a wonderful group of self-selected outdoor types interested in running through the countryside – and drinking local beer. Designated "hares" go out in advance and lay a trail with white lime powder "signs" through paths in the countryside, including traps and cutbacks designed to have all runners complete the course in roughly the same time. When I carried Jeremy in a backpack, we took the short loop. An award ceremony involving lots of beer follows each week's run. My buddy Jim acted as Hash Master and wore a mask with a rubber penis as the nose. After nearly two years of HHH, Deb and I garnered enough runs to earn ourselves pewter mugs and richly decorated bathrobes on our eventual departure from Java.

Let's Live in the Caribbean

"I call it the Margarita Road. It's the course your heart sets when you want to leave the past behind and start over someplace new and warm. Usually the path heads south to blue water and white sand, with any bumps along the way smoothed over by rum and tequila. It's not for everyone. This is a highway traveled mostly by runaways and drifters. I know, because I'm one of them."
— Anthony Lee Head, Driftwood: Stories from the Margarita Road

1988 brought the opportunity to move our young family to Barbados. An agriculture investment project needed me to help manage an agribusiness investment program in the English-speaking Eastern Caribbean. Our technical team was vetting and designing equity investment opportunities for a locally-established agricultural venture trust. We'd set up business investment deals, primarily equity, that helped the local economies. The trust invested in tropical fruit juices, cut flowers, and fresh fruit targeting the hospitality industry. After all, 50% of what every tourist spends, they spend on food and beverage!

This job meant that we moved to Barbados, a lovely island in the southern portion of the Caribbean Sea. Sounds idyllic, I'm sure, but the fact was that as overseas posts go, it was less welcoming than others. As contractors, at every overseas post one of the first things we learned was how warmly (or less so) accepted we were into the diplomatic circle of the US government. Some places simply needed us more than others. In Barbados, they didn't need us so much. There was less Embassy support for things like customs clearances, finding and leasing housing, making available furniture and appliances, and eventually there was a little less "inclusion" than we'd experienced in more out of the way postings.

Debbie set about making herself the MVP of the official community. She found, met, and charmed the US community social organizers. They became our friends. She organized and volunteered like nobody's business. We became "nearly" official members of the community. At one Easter party little Jeremy was surprised by the giant Easter Bunny – and didn't like it one bit. It put him completely off costumed giants.

Our house in Bridgetown was nice enough, a single-story house built in a "U" shape with an inner courtyard/garden patio. There was an empty field next door to us, which for a time caused some trouble with a peeping tom. We borrowed a large black dog and that solved <u>that</u> problem.

The weather was superb, and of course in just a few months Debbie's charm and value as a volunteer made us invaluable members of the international community. The Halloween Party at the Marine House was particularly memorable. The Marines had built their own spook house in the garage with boxes and sheets. Debbie tried to protect the little kids, including Jeremy, from getting their spines scared out of them – but failed. Brooms grabbing their feet and fire extinguishers spraying smoke left the kids screaming and running. Fully spooked.

That Easter, Debbie and I wanted to have an egg hunt in our living room for little Jeremy. We hid a dozen colored eggs in plain sight around the living room and went off to Easter mass. Upon our return, all the eggs were missing without a trace of colored shell. Our new Labrador puppy, however, was looking pleased and very plump. For the next several days, the back yard was dog-poop-decorated in lovely pastels.

While my office was in Bridgetown, Barbados, where the USAID offices were, my work required coordinating with a set of Island Advisors based in St. Kitts, Grenada, St. Vincent, St. Lucia, and Dominica. That meant overnight trips to these exotic and lovely places to keep tabs on and coordinate the investment efforts of our island advisors.

It turned out that the Hash House Harriers were alive and well in Barbados too! So, we connected and enjoyed the organized periodic outings to run and drink beer. When you move to a new community, HHH is an idea mechanism to self-select yourself into a group of like-minded people!

In the islands, you learn about rum. It's made from sugar cane. It's everyone's special beverage. You learn how to make a good rum punch. Use fine rum and whatever fresh fruit juice available; don't make them too sweet. Add ice and stir. The classic is "1 part sour (lime juice), 2 parts sweet (simple syrup), 3 parts strong (rum), 4 parts weak (ice). The final step is to grate some fresh nutmeg from Grenada on top. Yumm.

I had a chance to take diving lessons, which I did to get certified in scuba diving. I learned that I breathe a lot. Remember those good lungs? I was usually the first in the group to have to surface because I'd used my air up! For the duration of the dive, I had to sit in the rocking boat and wait for all the slow breathers to finish their dives. But the underwater world is a beautiful place to be weightless and explore. The water was warm so there was no need of any wetsuit. The government sank some ships off the calm west coast for sea habitat. What a beautiful place to dive!

Come Home to Raise the Kids

*"Do not tie yourself to any ideology in this infinite universe.
Explore fearlessly and live peacefully."*
– Nitin Namdeo

After living in Indonesia and then Barbados, Deb and I decided that it was best to move back to the U.S. to let the kids grow up a bit in their own culture. Some of Deb's childhood friends had a bad experience trying to rejoin the American culture after too long overseas. We certainly didn't want that to happen to our kid, Jeremy!

We rented a house in downtown Bethesda, MD from where Deb could drop me at DC's new metro in the morning and collect me in the evening.

I again recreated my professional self and rejoined a fast-moving corporate environment in the world of consulting firms known informally as the "beltway bandits." Now, I had some overseas leadership under my belt and a better sense of what it took to plan and execute an economic development project in a challenging environment.

My work life became a balance of short-term assignments to Bangladesh and Pakistan, Haiti and Cote d'Ivoire, etc. I travelled to China to do a study for the USDA & the

U.S. Produce industry on the feasibility of American fresh fruit and vegetable exports to China. The simplified answer: Yes, but with a tricky market chain, a tricky market in the mega-cities, a tricky evolving set of policy constraints as China began to open its markets to imported products. For marketing details, check with the produce marketing association.

On another work trip, I was privileged to visit Peshawar, Pakistan where our field team was working Afghanistan cross-border community development – think school and bridge construction. It was understandably challenging work for our team. Americans didn't cross the border; there was a war going on between Russia and various militant groups fighting for control of the country.

Our American team sent Afghans and Pakistani staff to identify culverts, community gardens, etc. to repair and support. Our American staff were very stressed. Those who were close to the local culture became aware of various declared enemies of the fight who would disappear, essentially be cut into small pieces and spread in the nearby Hindu Kush no man's land. There was a time when our staff were asked to identify anyone giving them a hard time, suggesting that their names could be added to a Russian ally list – and thereafter be "disappeared."

I visited the Northwest Frontier Territory where tribal law, not national, is the governing rule. One step off the paved road meant that tribal law ruled. One village became famous and profitable as a gun manufacturing and sales center souvenirs. Guns from historic replicas of WWII era Luger pistols to shoulder-mounted grenade launchers. Even back in Peshawar, the market offered single-fire 22 shell ball-point pens. Ignorant American tourists were routinely caught at the airport trying to take those out of the country. I saw buttons cut off Soviet military uniforms for sale. I bought a small Soviet military cap as a souvenir for my young son. Inside was the original owner's name written in Cyrillic.

Closer to home, I had an eventful visit to the Caribbean. My overnight stay in St. Lucia was interrupted in the middle of the night when I woke up with a sharp pain in my ear. At first, I thought it was due to my flight the day before. I took an antihistamine and chewed gum, pinched my nose and tried to "blow" my ear pressure right. And then a bit of blood leaked from my ear and the pain stopped. The next morning, I decided to try the air travel home. I figured it was preferable to risk the altitude travel to get medical treatment stateside than to seek it locally. At altitude and pressure, would my brain implode or try to come out my ear through a busted eardrum? But the trip home was fine, and I had no more pain.

A few weeks later, facing an assignment in Indonesia, I decided to visit a doctor. The ENT expert was very good. He first said that he couldn't quite see the eardrum to examine it. He needed to move some blood clot first. Then he showed me what he had removed. His tweezers held a perfectly formed beetle with pincers on the front end. It had apparently gotten lodged in my ear canal while I slept, then tried to bite its way out, eventually drowning in my blood. The ENT gave me some eardrops to use and said it was good that I had visited him. If left there, the dead beetle would have caused an infection.

Eventually Deb and I bought a small house in Silver Spring, with a swing set in the backyard for Jeremy. We became homeowners!

A year later, Deb decided that in fact we should live in Bethesda, not Silver Spring, and she found us an affordable brick bungalow there with a great magnolia tree in front. I made her promise that we would never again buy and then sell a house within a year. She agreed. We haven't.

Bethesda was a great match for our young family. We pulled up the ugly green wall-to-wall carpet, tore down the gauze curtains and the plastic swinging bar doors to the kitchen, redid the hardwood floors and in 1990 moved into our forever home. Nicole was born in a nearby hospital.

That house in Bethesda is still home (in 2021). Now we call it our retirement home.

I Never Had a Farm in Africa

"Be bold and mighty forces will come to your aid."
\- Goethe

The chance to move back to Africa eventually came at the consulting firm in 1992, I had an opportunity to draft a winning proposal for a project in Kenya – and to put myself on it as Chief of Party. If we won, our family would move there and I'd run the project. We did, we did, and I did.

Nairobi, Kenya was the new post for the (now) family of four. Back to driving on the left side of the road, steering wheel on the right, stick shift with the left hand. The new project was the Kenya Export Development Project (KEDS) or as I said "KEDS, the project, not the shoe." I rented office space around the corner from the famous Norfolk Hotel. Teddy Roosevelt hunted lions back in the day from the Norfolk Hotel front patio. My mother-in-law during a visit noted that the front patio was perhaps the nicest place in the world to sit and sip a cold draft beer. She also had made that comment in Bali.

I hired a team of local program and administrative professionals, and set up shop, developed a work plan and identified our institutional partners. The purpose of the project was to promote and diversify Kenya's exports, thereby earning foreign exchange and creating sustainable jobs for small horticulture farmers and exporters.

For living in the Horn of Africa, Debbie and I found housing to rent, got the kids into the International School of Kenya, made new friends, and established ourselves anew within a functioning social circle that included the development set and diplomats, but also business leaders who managed regional offices. Things like electricity and telephone lines were more complicated than in the first world. But we found our way.

Friends invited us to join them at exclusive Muthaiga Country Club New Year's Parties. Other friends organized regular Sunday afternoon gatherings at a Tex-Mex restaurant that they managed where we feasted on off-the-menu "'Migas" and sampled shots from a *bandoliered* waitress who wore shot glasses instead of bullets, with house-brand tequila bottles in hip holsters. This is where I learned to lick the salt from Deb's clavicle, shoot the tequila shot, then bite the lime.

Those restaurant managers threw memorable parties. The *Prawns at Dawn* Party at their residence began at 5 am. Gates were locked at the crack of dawn. Lanterns lined the walkway around to the back yard. Tents were set up covering tables and chairs. Centerpieces featured pitchers of bloody mary and the raw materials for mimosas. Prawns were served seven or eight ways. At sunrise, we walked a loop around the yard and danced to a live band until about 10 am when we straggled home for naps.

The host also organized a "mystery birthday day" for his wife, to which we were invited, an exclusive invitation since we would complete the birthday party foursome. Birthday girl picked us up in a London cab at 7:30 am and we drove to the country club to find her partner outside the restaurant. He acted like the reservation was messed up and suggested we return to their house instead for breakfast. Departing the club, our driver noted that he had to register at the corner of the parking lot. We were dropped off next to a fairway with a view of the area's tea plantations. There was a table set up for us, decorated with roses and balloons, for our full breakfast. We were serenaded by a lovely woman vocalist and her guitarist.

Then the two ladies departed in the cab for a beauty shop arranged visit for "mani" and "pedi" – with more champagne and roses surrounding them; he and I headed to add final touches to the late morning break by the river below their house. After the women joined us there for bloody marys, we carried our drinks in the cab to a southern suburb restaurant that featured a Kenyan lunch feast with a cultural show. Debbie "rested her head" on her arms after lunch for a little rest and recuperation.

In the afternoon, we headed to another suburb's hotel complex where our organizer friend worked. As the three of us presented ourselves at Reception, they gave us keys to the Presidential Suite where we found, what else, roses and champagne. Afternoon naps ensued. We met him for dinner at a Japanese restaurant in the complex where the frying food sent Debbie back to our room for more rest and relief. I persevered through a brief casino visit before calling it a night myself. The next morning after breakfast the London taxi delivered us home. Naps.

For <u>my</u> next birthday, Deb planned a 24-hour special surprise day for me. At the Nairobi airport that morning I learned that we were flying to Mombasa on the coast. On check-in at our beach hotel we bumped into our friend and previously Birthday Girl. That evening we four dined on lobster with our bare toes wiggling in the white sand, then capped off the evening with a dinner cruise on the Indian Ocean on a traditional dhow under a full moon.

The KEDS project's timing was fortuitous. Too often a development project is designed but by the time we get to implementation, economic conditions have changed, and the project implementation becomes more challenging.

In this case, the timing turned out great. The old President, Daniel Arup Moi, was now allowing multi-party democracy and you could feel the tide turning. Conversations about changes in the government were increasingly happening, albeit in low voices in people's back gardens. The Central Bank reformed and liberalized foreign exchange – exporters could earn – and retain - forex! Several politically connected commercial banks closed. A younger generation of bureaucrats assumed leadership of the Ministries of

Agriculture and Commerce. It was a GOOD time to lead an export development program!

Kenya is home to some of the world's most incredible game parks. Our favorite place was in the country's southwest Rift Valley, a park known as Masai Mara. We drove our own car, used a compass touring the immense and unfenced area, and stayed in what were described as luxury tented camps that boasted all the amenities of home including flush toilets, and electricity!

Three game drives per day in an open-topped Land Rover with a knowledgeable guide brought us closer to the zebra and antelopes, elephants and giraffes, hippos and hyenas, and on special days the big cats and crocs. We were fortunate to time one visit with the great migration of the wildebeest, that I liked to refer to as the "Guenette Gnus." Another visit gifted us a cheetah

 hunting a lone antelope, two hours of silent stealth through the dry grass, followed by five seconds of furious action, culminating in another cheetah lesson in nature. There's a lyric in a children's song that goes something like "I'm not bad, I'm just hungry."

When conditions are right, vast numbers of the "lesser" flamingoes congregate to feed on the special algae growing at Lake Nakuru a few hours' drive north of Nairobi. Lesser flamingos are white at birth, but after enough time on this diet the algae's pigments filter

into the birds' feathers, tinting them a dashing pink with red highlights. It's a shockingly beautiful view to see these birds gathered by the thousands. When our group tried to have a picnic lunch out of the backs of our cars, however, we were bothered by aggressive baboons. Despite our making loud noises and slapping our chests as a show of power, they kept circling around us wanting our food. In the end, we packed up and moved elsewhere to have our lunch.

Beautiful Lake Naivasha lies just over an hour's drive north of Nairobi. It's the lake that drives Kenya's tropical flower export industry. The lake is home to hippos, very dangerous animals that we would get a close look at from small boats. On one visit with our son Jeremy, the three of us were dropped off at a small island for an hour visit that was, we were assured, quite safe since there were no predator cats there. To our surprise however, we did happen on a herd of water buffalo who became agitated by our presence. We withdrew to the pier and awaited our prearranged pick-up.

We came to love a small private game reserve near Mount Kenya called Sweetwaters. Like many places in Kenya, it has a colorful past. A large company established it as a reserve in 1988 for black rhino. Over time it expanded to 90,000 acres. As a private reserve, it can offer night game drives, a thrilling experience for all. In our open-top Rover one night we found giant leopards. I say giant because I swear, they were 7-feet long. They were lounging comfortably, 4-5 of them as we approached and paused alongside them. Magnificent and thrilling to see these majestic cats up close.

A notorious Middle Eastern weapons dealer of some fame in the 1970's and 80's at some point acquired this lovely corner of the earth. He built an opulent residence for himself featuring two swimming pools and a tennis court, "his" and "her" main bedrooms and two guest rooms; eventually several outbuildings added six more rooms. The story goes that in the high-flying earlier days of colonial Kenya, made famous by the book "White Mischief" he lost the residence to the owner of a hotel chain in a high stakes card game.

For expats living in Nairobi, the attraction was to organize a murder mystery weekend there and rent out the whole place with eight couples. The great dining room featured a canoe near the ceiling posed on pulleys. The rumor went that in earlier times, the canoe could be lowered by rope for "dessert," revealing a naked Lufthansa stewardess "wearing" the various cheeses and sweet choices. The living room furniture was greatly oversized, prompting SNL references to Gilda Radnor's little girl character in a frilly dress rocking her legs which didn't reach the floor. Real lion and zebra skins were scattered about the floors.

Outside, we installed a slip-n-slide for exercise. We organized teams for a scavenger hunt, on which we found the elephant shit but didn't win the contest. When our land-rover got stuck in an aardvark, ant-eater hole on the track, British military who were on exercises pulled us out with their 10-ton Bedford truck.

For the special murder mystery weekend, we drew straws to see who would get "his" or "her" bedroom. Debbie and I got lucky and got "his." We found the giant canopy bed large enough to lie down on it with our heads in opposite corners – and our feet didn't meet in the middle! There is a group photo somewhere of all sixteen of us perched on this bed. The attached bath was no less oversized; there's also a photo of all of us in the bathtub, with giant elephant tusks arching over the tub. Yes, we all fit into the tub – fully-clothed mind you. I still have my branded sweater vest that I earned as the Weekend MVP.

From Southern Kenya, the highest point in Africa, Mount Kilimanjaro looms. Evidently it was once "ceded" from the Queen of England to the German Kaiser, so the Kenya southern border cuts a loop north around the mountain, leaving it laying wholly in

Tanzania. Those living in East Africa hear tales of summiting Mount Kilimanjaro, the drama and beauty, the grit, and the altitude sickness.

But climbing it is "possible" from Nairobi if one organizes a group. A friend of mine was organizing a group and I bought into the service package and tagged along. Debbie wasn't interested. We had guides, porters to carry our stuff, and a cook to prep evening meals and box lunches. We spent an incredible six days on the mountain, four going up and two coming down. Most days were a long walk of a few miles, gaining another kilometer in altitude, with a brown bag lunch break. Nights we stayed in 3-person Norwegian-constructed A-frames with our sleeping bags on foam pads. A larger A-frame served as the dining hall for travelling teams. As we ascended the mountain, the temperature dropped. I dressed in all my necessary layers and hung a water bottle on a rope around my neck.

Our guides emphasized slow and steady, pushing liquids and taking a full day to reach the night's campsite. The "easy" route is a long walk but doesn't require technical climbing or crampons. You just must be able to walk waaaay up, which we did.

The summit of Mount Kilimanjaro at just over 19,000 feet above sea level, is stunning. You find yourself above the clouds in clear sunshine but walking beside glaciers. 100 baby steps of heavy breathing followed by a brief rest leaning on our walking sticks. I signed the book at the summit, in pencil, since pens froze.

As my birthday present and our going away from Kenya present, Deb and I bought ourselves another priceless experience – a sunrise flight around the peak of Mount Kenya. We again visited the beautiful Mount Kenya Safari Club known for peacocks wandering the grounds, hotel rooms with views of Mount Kenya, fireplaces in the rooms that staff light for you in the evening, and a separate dining area and meals for children. So classy! We discussed over a cocktail the flying possibility with an ex-Navy pilot who owned an open-cockpit biplane.

Taking off from a grass airstrip in the predawn darkness, we crammed into the front cockpit and flew at sunrise around the peak of Mount Kenya wearing leather jackets, goggles, and silk scarves, warmed by the engine and prop wash. The pilot spoke over the headphones, but  most of the time we listened to the soundtrack from "Out of Africa."

The pilot who owns the plane rode in the "back" cockpit. We watched waterbuck gamboling in the glacier melt streams washing down from the summit. And the sun rose over the Indian Ocean in the direction of Mombasa. From above the clouds, we could see Mount Kilimanjaro not too far to the south, the highest peak in Africa, waving goodbye to us.

Come Home to Raise the Parents

"What matters most is how well you walk through the fire."
– Charles Bukowski

By summer 1996, it was apparent that it was time to return to the U.S. The KEDS project was ending and that meant returning to the consulting firm's Bethesda, MD headquarters - and that meant again reinventing myself professionally.

My father had passed away and our remaining three parents were aging. The kids, Jeremy and Nicole, needed to reinsert themselves into their home culture. Jeremy was eleven by now and showed the wisdom of ages when coming home from his new school one evening he remarked that "Kids here - they don't know how lucky they are."

We hung with my in-laws a few months until our rented house was vacant and available for us to move into. I still love that I was friends with Bob and Rosemary since before I met Deb, but it was close quarters until we could move back "home." I arranged a few overseas trips for myself during this "just a bit crowded" time.

The next four years were fabulous in terms of growing my resume. I did the classic U.S.-based international development work consisting largely of three pots of work to fill my timesheet: paid consulting assignments all over the developing world, new business development efforts writing winning proposals, and managing overseas projects.

My travels included faraway places as diverse as Bangladesh, Zambia, Haiti, and Rwanda (where I stayed at THAT hotel popularized in cinema). In these countries each airport is a surprise. You go in brave and bold, and hustle and hassle your way through to the other side.

Paul Guenette

Eastern Europe was new for me after the iron curtain fell. Their airports were still figuring out how to receive foreign visitors. At one airport, arriving exhausted passengers were milling about, unsure of which lines to join for visa formalities. I joined a line. After investing a half hour in my queue, I learned that it was in fact a visa line, good, but the visa line that required you to give them a photo! I didn't want to switch lines now. But lo! I had an old library card in my wallet with a photo sealed in plastic! Using my teeth, I freed that photo just in time to get my new Romanian visa.

While departing from Maputo, Mozambique after a work visit, all boarding travelers were asked to point out and claim their checked bags before they were stowed. Mine weren't there. They had lost my luggage between check-in and boarding. My suitcase took a round-about trip home to the states and eventually caught up to me.

I led a small team of economists on a job in Lesotho, the Kingdom in the Sky surrounded and dominated by South Africa. One of the Economists was less experienced than the others. At one of the city's several restaurants for dinner, this guy began by asking the waiter if they served non-alcoholic beer. The waiter was very puzzled, and to clarify, he explained that he wanted beer without any alcohol in it. We shouted down our consultant dissuading him and bringing him back to reality – or so we thought. Moments later, the waiter brought us glasses of ice water. Our Economist piped up and asked the waiter, "Do you boil your ice?" Now the waiter was convinced that this guy was really messing with him. He laughed at the joke and walked away.

Among my most memorable work trips was to the Democratic Republic of the Congo, formerly Zaire. I was managing a start-up team comprised of Congolese development managers, paired with former Peace Corps volunteers who had lived in, and thus could speak local language and were comfortable with customs and cultures, in three outposts spread across this huge country.

We were building a network of professionals to manage small grants to local non-profits, think building schools and bridges, improving roads, and water sources.

I stayed a nice Kinshasa hotel, but this was when the country had just freed itself from one despot and added another, his son. The national currency was in free fall. The hotel cashier was in a plexiglass booth piled floor to ceiling with Central Bank bundles tied into packets of a million *Zaires* sealed with a stamped piece of lead. A hundred U.S. dollars got you several tied bales of cash. The trick was not to break the leaded seal so that you could make purchases "by the million." Cashing several hundred dollars meant that you had to carry away the local currency in a small duffle bag.

Cellphones were new and popular, most businessmen carried three to access the three separate services, but ring tones were all the same, making for high comedy when someone in a restaurant got a call – and everyone began checking their three phones to see if it was for them.

My room had a view of the Congo River, and across the river, the neighboring country's capitol, Brazzaville, which was still at civil war. The view from my room at night featured red tracers as fighting raged on just a river away.

We didn't leave the big city on that trip but numerous times we had our car stopped by young men brandishing large weapons at homemade informal roadblocks. When one of our vehicles was stolen, our staff got a tip that we could recover it near the university. It had just been used for joyriding until it ran out of gas.

My trip home was even more "special" than my stay had been I flew Air Zaire from Kinshasa east to Bukavu (where I stepped briefly onto the tarmac to listen for ongoing fighting) before connecting north to Entebbe, Uganda (known for the Israeli commandoes' rescue of a terrorist highjacked plane). I then flew

Air Kenya east to Nairobi (where the U.S. Embassy had been recently bombed) and changed to a northbound Swiss Air flight to Geneva.

Ah, Europe, right? I had to catch a Swiss Air domestic flight from Geneva to Zurich for my connection to the U.S. I couldn't help but notice that my tired sun-burned body stood out in my dusty Africa clothing among a planeload of white Swiss businessmen all in dark suits. As we neared landing in Zurich, the plane began to "yaw," is that the right word? It was rotating left and right rather violently. From my left window seat, I saw the wing tip come within 10 feet of the tarmac while the right wing aimed at the sky. The pilot aborted the landing suddenly, oxygen masks dropped, and several overhead bins spilled their luggage as the roar of the gunned engines drowned out some polite gasps (them) and a nice squeal (me). Hell no! I've been working in Congo and flown through Uganda and Kenya to get here. I will NOT die in a fiery crash in Switzerland with all these old suited-up white guys.

After we leveled off, the pilot came on with his best Chuck Yaeger voice to inform us that we'd hit a little turbulence from the 747 landing before us and that we'd just take another lap around and try again.

In 2000, when I got a call from a large consulting firm's recruiter asking me if I could recommend anyone for an agribusiness development position in Deloitte's Washington office, I naively commented that maybe I'd be interested myself. Of course, that was exactly what they'd hoped would happen. I'd grown tired of my current supervisor and the attraction of a career move was strong. Though I'd been with them16 years and worked all over the world so I didn't take leaving them lightly. I went to Human Resources and asked what proper protocol was. I wanted to leave correctly.

The best thing about my new job was having a boss in the next country! Among my favorite bosses anywhere, this wonderful woman ran the agribusiness team from Guelph, just outside Toronto, Canada. She came to D.C. a half dozen times a year, and I went to Canada 3-4 times a year. I really enjoyed the entrepreneurial work and I reveled in the strategy of "marrying" the consulting firm's reputation in financial services with the admittedly Canada-based agribusiness to compete and win U.S. government contracts.

In 2006, my career life changed again. A prominent non-profit development organization called with an offer that I couldn't refuse. They wanted me to help manage a growing portfolio of development programs in Africa. What a wonderful completion of the circle. I could return to Africa!

I did some of my career's best work there. After managing the Africa portfolio, we reorganized our management structure and I co-managed the Agribusiness practice, getting my chops in food security via improved value chain performance.

I loved managing (and visiting) the projects in Egypt – where the pyramids of Giza are in the suburbs of Cairo. You could see them from the project office restroom if you stuck your head out the window. The great pyramid was the tallest building in the world for 4,000 years. Time curves.

And managing the program in Ghana was like coming "home" to my Peace Corps experience. Ghana extends from Accra and the sea in the south, through rice-rich highlands, all the way north to Tamale which is classically Sahelian with baobab trees, millet and sorghum. There are even a few Fulani tribes, "my" people.

It was amazing to lead our Board of Directors on a few overseas trips to educate them as to how our field projects really worked. I led them to Kenya and Tanzania on one trip, showing them my old stomping ground and our programs helping farmers connect to markets and raise their productivity and resilience.

Another fun board of director's visit was flying south to the Caribbean for a visit to Jamaica. Our program there was modernizing agriculture, strengthening indigenous market information systems, and working with youth as change-leaders in their rural agricultural systems. I did manage to add in a visit to Bob Marley's old digs – on his birthday as it turns out – which opened a few of the directors' eyes (and noses) to the local culture of this joyful people.

Ethiopia is a proud people and country, never colonized. They successfully fought off the Italians for years. They have a portion of the rift valley but haven't been able to capitalize on the country's physical beauty with tourism for reasons of weak governance. Some colleagues and I were there staffing and planning a new rural agriculture improvement project.

We took a weekend to visit Ethiopia's northern city of Axum. Centuries ago, it was a port city. Now it's bone dry, far from any sea, and the soil is exhausted and bare. All Ethiopian emperors for 3,000 years had been crowned here through Haile Selassie who died in 1975. It emits an Old Testament atmosphere. An old woman rode sidesaddle on a small donkey. The ruins are being explored to reveal the palace of the Queen of Sheba. A lone priest lives his life in isolation, caring for the locked cabinet which purportedly holds the Ark of the Covenant.

I flew into South Sudan just after they'd declared independence. The newly independent South Sudan airport in Juba was a ruin. The luggage claim area was accessible to the public by stepping over a low wall – the glass was missing. My greeter stepped in to help me with luggage and I followed him out by stepping through the wall.

My "hotel room" in Juba was half of a twenty-foot container. It was over 100 degrees all the time, but my "room" featured a tiny air-conditioner stuck to the wall which made it worth the $100/night cost (payable in cash in advance). My bed was flat against the drywall that split the container in two. Someone else's bed was on the other side of that drywall, in their room. All meals were served in the nearby "dining tent" that posted a sign at the entrance flap "No weapons inside." My other stops on that trip were in two aptly named places called Wow and Yei (pronounced "yay!") They were less equipped for visitors than Juba.

In Serbia, we had some government VIPs visiting a beneficiary farm. After the visit to look over the farmer's field, the farmer & I marched straight up a steep hill to the barn while the VIPs took the slower switchback trail. We entered the barn first of course and the farmer pulled back a burlap cloth to reveal some shot glasses and his homemade slivovitz, the local plum brandy. We crossed ourselves, did the shots & he covered it all back over with the burlap. Then the VIPs arrived for the speeches – and were not offered shots. Hmmm.

I also enjoyed my visit to Viet Nam, happily my first, having successfully avoided visiting in 1973. I sought out the old bar made famous by reporters during the Viet Nam War. I was hoping to speak French, but English is *de rigeur*, only a few elderly people still spoke French. The fertility of the soil and abundance of water made for very different approaches to farming than can be done in the dryer Sahel. In the central highlands, our projects were guiding thousands of small farmers into more productive coffee farming, improving varieties, pruning, and post-harvest treatments to produce high-grade Arabica specialty coffee. Their dedication to the task and their work ethic impressed me mightily. The domestic flights on Viet Nam Air were very much a first-world experience. This country sure knew how to get things done.

Another of the special countries to which my work brought me was Lebanon. I marveled at the culture, speaking Arabic, French, and English all during a single meal at a fabulous restaurant. My luggage had gotten misdirected upon arrival – but there was a modern department store just down the road in Beirut – where I could buy slacks and a dress shirt.

On a coastal highway drive to the north, we stopped in the small fishing village of Byblos. It's a magical place, one of the oldest continually inhabited cities in the world, where it is said that Christ walked the beach. Byblos was already old when the Crusaders conquered it. Byblos means "papyrus" stemming from its ancient exports of papyrus – which in turn lent its name to the word "bible." That's ancient.

Then when the non-profit's VP Public Relations retired back in our DC-based headquarters, the President tapped me for VP Communications. This role felt like I'd come full circle to my communication and theatre roots. I *knew* first-hand the technical and field content, and I *knew* from experience the messaging that we should put out to the world. With a small team of technicians, that's what we did!

A career high came with the responsibility for coordinating our global strategy in 2014. Two years later, the board asked me to be Acting President and CEO while they searched for a replacement.

I finished my storied career there as Chief Communications Officer, and formally retired at the end of 2019.

A Kick in the Crotch

*"You never really know how strong you are until being
strong is the only choice you have."*
– Bob Marley

My journey with prostate cancer began in March 2008 with a routine annual physical. My blood test among other things noted a slightly elevated PSA. The doctor told me that while it wasn't an emergency, that I should visit a Urologist, and that I'd probably bought myself a biopsy.

Indeed. The biopsy led to more tests including a CT scan, and within weeks culminated in "Robotically-assisted laparoscopic radical prostatectomy with lymph node dissection." The cancer strength in such matters is measured by the Gleason Score on a scale of one to ten, with low scores in your favor. Ever the high achiever, mine scored a ten.

Within a few months, my PSA dropped to undetectable though, suggesting that the surgery had "gotten it." Joy was short-lived. Within a year, my PSA count had risen again to the point where we decided that those little cancer beasts were most likely in the prostate bed, and a targeted radiation could kick it out once and for all.

We scheduled radiation treatments, impressive-sounding Image-Guided Radiation Therapy. At 200 rads a pop it would total 7400 rads, enough I'm sure to develop or ruin at least a few rolls of film. Again, as evidence of treatment success, my PSA became undetectable!

We visited that Urologist quarterly (I say "we" since Debbie came to every one of them with me.) And each time a blood test confirmed the glorious state of "undetectable" leading to what became a tradition of martini celebrations.

119

These quarterly festivities carried on for three years. At this stage the Urologist guardedly voiced the opinion that with an aggressive cancer like this to have not reoccurred in three years likely meant that we indeed had zapped it for good with the radiation. Of course, that jinxed it, and our next visit ran a little long as they rechecked the blood sample before the doctor gave us the bad news that "it's baaaack!"

We dropped the Urologist in January 2013 and got ourselves a sharp Oncologist, connected to a strong local medical network. Thus began my participation in a series of clinical trials. One of the benefits was that annually we'd run a full battery of tests (Blood & urine lab work, CT w/ contrast abdomen & pelvis scan; nuclear medicine whole body bone scan). "Passing the tests" made us feel at least a little better, while on a quarterly visit we watched the PSA rise slowly for two years.

Then in December 2014 the CT annual scans identified some suspicious soft tissue thickening the bladder wall. This led to a fine needle biopsy of the suspect swell (needle approaching from the BACK, mind you) which showed the bladder wall positive for prostate cancer. We'd already removed the prostate, and then radiated the prostate bed, so the cancer has apparently left the room. It could be anywhere in my body. Elvis is no longer in the house!

Since I'd already maxed out on radiation to the abdomen, this meant my new Rx was "double continuous androgen deprivation therapy" known more commonly on the street as "hormone therapy." Essentially, since prostate cancer feeds off testosterone, we want to starve it into submission by stopping my body from producing my joy juice.

Again, I lucked out on this clinical trial and got into the arm of the study using Casodex and Eligard. The other arm of the study apparently didn't go so well. Patients had riotous side effects.

Within a month, my PSA reading had returned to the golden status of "undetectable."

At my next annual battery of tests, the CT scan now gloriously showed a <u>resolution</u> of the thickening in my bladder wall that we'd discovered a year earlier. The double continuous androgen deprivation therapy was working! I'll be on these two medications for life.

Update to 2021, and the 3-month visits are almost routine. Almost. You schedule, you pop in for a blood draw to hopefully show PSA still undetectable and to get a shot of slow-dissolving Eligard in the tummy. I say routine since the schedule is regular. There's always apprehension waiting a day for the lab test results. Are the meds continuing to work? As of 2021 this magical combo has been working to suppress my Stage IV prostate cancer for six years.

And counting. At some point some nasty cancer cells will morph and figure a way around these medications. At that stage we'll add something new to chase down those nasties. So, the clinical trial nurse emails me the good news when the PSA test results come in, and Debbie and I can breathe easily for the time being. We have the follow-up visit with the Oncologist, but since the PSA is still undetectable it's an easy visit. Then typically, Deb and I celebrate with martinis. And the next three-month period begins.

What Happened to "My" Village?

"Man cannot discover new oceans unless he has the
courage to lose sight of the shore."
- Andre Gide

40 Years after joining the Peace Corps, I returned to the small African village in the Sahara Desert where I began my career in international development. Social ties are indeed the ties that bind. Because of a "little brother" who was educated, our shared tribal identity brought us together years later, leading to a warm reunion that made an insightful trip back to the village possible.

In 2004, I was called to Dakar, Senegal to help the African Union work on a piece of the Comprehensive African Agricultural Development Plan. While in Dakar I always used my African name and local language. This led to a contact in the neighboring hotel who put me in touch with my little brother from the village.

My "little brother" was now a PhD medical doctor managing country-wide health programs for an American consulting firm funded by the US government. We only had time for a cup of tea visit but with the wonders of communications technology, he had me speak briefly on his mobile phone with our "mother" back in the village. My weak Pulaar quickly failed me but I was able to thank her for taking good care of me so long ago, remind her that she's my mother, and tell her that I love her. I promised my brother that next time through Senegal I'd take more time and we could visit the village together.

Now jump ten years to 2014, when I travelled to Senegal to speak at the opening of a West Africa regional rice mechanization project. I checked in with my brother by email to learn that his two children were both doing well and living in the states now but that our "mother" had passed away last October. We agreed that after my meetings in Dakar we would drive with his wife back to the

123

village for an Independence Day weekend visit. What a chance to see the village which nearly forty years ago taught me so much about humanity thriving in a very harsh environment and the people who taught me about sincere generosity amid abject poverty. The place which so deeply touched me that it launched my lifetime of international rural development. What would I find?

On the eve of our trip from the capital city, Dakar, I met up with my brother at my hotel. Dakar's population had grown by five times to five million. A new highway smoothly delivers traffic from the airport to downtown along the beach. Hotels and restaurants had sprung up. Happily, I noted that while the city has grown to encompass the airport and extend to nearby Ngor, the developers managed to conserve Soumbedioune, the beach-based fishing port and market. From my hotel roof I could watch the fishermen leave at sunrise in their brightly colored boats, to return with fresh fish to sell in the mid-afternoon.

It was an eight-hour drive to my village now, whereas previously it was a two-day trip by bush taxi. We left Dakar on a divided toll-way highway cruising 150 miles north to Saint-Louis, then headed east 200 miles, first on newly paved roads then on remnants of the old broken paved road. The milestone markers alerted us 80 kilometers before and counted down to Pété. Nice to have my brother as tour guide. Then at kilometer 0, a big sign announced the village of Pété.

Since I was last here in 1976, the village had grown from 1,200 to 6,000 residents. It now reaches and has crossed the paved road. The intersection is crowded with people and vehicles, stores, and a taxi station. Business is prospering. Pété is incorporated into a city now and has an elected Mayor, though the chief and elders still exist for consultation.

The old open well is capped and four others dug. Water is piped throughout the village and into many homes. Women no longer pull it up 25 meters by hand and carry it on their heads to the family compounds. Rice is king now, strengthened by sophisticated irrigation from the river and several major dams. Millet and sorghum cultivation are down. Available water means women have time and the means to garden fresh vegetables. Neighborhood gardens grow onions, tomatoes, carrots, pumpkin, *bissap*, and herbs. Farmers in the region sell tons of onions and tomatoes contributing to the country's recent production surge. Nationally, Senegal now supplies its domestic need for vegetables eight months of the year.

Schools have sprung up in the village. Where forty years ago there were two classrooms, now there are twelve. There are two primary schools now, plus a junior high and a high school. When my brother was small and I helped build the village's second classroom, he had to move to Saint-Louis in order to attend high school. I've always seen energy in youth, but this appeared to demonstrate education as an igniter, a catalyst that incites a willingness and ability to change.

The new larger post office has opened. There are two radio stations that broadcast regionally, including evening news in Pulaar, the local language. A small dispensary has been upgraded with a resident doctor and across the paved road, there's a newly constructed hospital about to open. There are businesses along the paved road where before there was nothing but open sand: a metal-working shop, a hair salon, multiple general stores, grocery markets and a taxi station.

We took an evening stroll at the edge of the village. We met women returning from their neighborhood gardens carrying fresh onions, tomatoes, greens, and eggplant. Some are even using drip irrigation. At sunset I went up onto the flat roof to appreciate the breeze during evening prayers. It's calm but I could hear children playing and singing. A little toddler came up the steps to visit me, chatting away in Pulaar. I kept writing. She sat beside me and kept talking despite my non-comprehending half-answers. I could feel the relaxed pace of the village evening seeping into me.

Okay, these will sound mundane, but remember I lived here long ago when all were mud huts, only one metal roof. There was one open well and one car in this little village.

NOW...Electricity running to the homes, without a generator. Electric plugs and lights. I had an electric fan in my room to help me sleep. A half dozen capped wells and a water tower mean water can be piped all over the village. I can receive and send emails from Pété on my smartphone. I can Tweet! I charged my iPhone and iPad. And I had a real flush toilet attached to my bedroom! The mundane is easy to take for granted unless you don't have it. I slept in my village that night. And I slept well.

Friday being dress-up day, I wore my decorative boubou much to the appreciation of the villagers. They loved my saying in Pulaar "Today is Friday" which needed no more justification. Since Friday is their religious day, it's the equivalent of our own "dress-up Sunday." We were visited on the veranda by an articulate young man who runs one of the radio stations. We filled him in on the story of volunteer returned and he invited us to stop by the station later for an interview.

I received a driving tour of the village during which I guiltily appreciated the car's air-conditioning. We visited the cemetery and paid our respects to our departed parents. Then we drove north on an improved road to see the southern branch of the Senegal River. It looked as inviting as ever. The show-off moment however was a solid modern bridge crossing to the north where carved-out log canoes used to ferry people across. There are still a few of the wooden canoes nearby used by fishermen.

We swung by the radio station and joined a journalism workshop that the station had organized for a group of high school students.

We were interviewed in front of the group, advised them to study hard, seek adventure that stirs their hearts, and to take the opportunities that present themselves. Then my brother headed to the mosque and I retired to the cool of my room for my own prayers.

That evening, in Pulaar, I heard our radio interview. I can follow enough Pulaar to hear him tell my story of the returned Peace Corps volunteer who traveled the world and then returned with his brother from here. The family seated around me listening to the radio under the stars exclaimed at my fame. They are truly touched that I made it back to visit them.

Saturday was just as hot, reaching 110 again, but I've mastered the art of frequent cool showers. Drying off isn't necessary in this oven-like heat; just wait a few minutes. We received visits from villagers who heard on the evening news of my return. Many I couldn't recognize, couldn't remember their names, but many remembered mine - as Mamadou Anne. Someone told the story of my playing my electric guitar and when I didn't want to play, I'd tell them the guitar was asleep. We laughed and remembered being young.

Then I got pleasantly shocked yet again. Mamadou Ka, the first Peace Corps volunteer stationed here since my stay 40 years earlier, dropped by. His Pulaar is masterful, he's been working on health and nutrition training of village teachers for two years. They incorporate his lessons into their own and hundreds of children are healthier for it. He came by with another young American who will replace him here. We posed for a photo of American support, past, present, and future.

Our "Young Americans" visit was too short. We told our stories to each other and tried to map out next steps for this wonderful place that has touched our lives. A credit union? A women's coop?

School gardens? Our English flowed like the river rapids, freed from working deep into our third language.

The veterans coached the new arrival. Push the water. Drink before you get thirsty. Stay out of the sun. Seek the shade. Cover up. Slow down. We warned him of the hot, dry season and its dangers, but reminded him of the glory of the rainy season when the desert blooms into a prairie and all the animals have babies. The cows give milk!

My village brother received a phone call on his cell from his daughter. She completed her nursing degree in Minnesota then moved to Atlanta and found a job. With a father's pride he passes me the phone and says, "She speaks perfect English!" And she does. She's saving up her annual leave for a trip back home. We exchange contacts.

I'm so excited, I try calling my wife Debbie in Bethesda from my hut on my iPhone. The call goes right through and she picks up. She says she stopped worrying when she got my email that the village had electricity and that I'd bought a case of bottled water. She hears my tales of surprise and joy and says "Honey, that's sounds so wonderful. There are stories of trips back to Africa that are so disappointing. You should write this story." Yea, I should.

Orion proudly arches

Orion proudly arches
Near the setting moon boldly sets his aim

Seeking star answers
My soul searching dark desert skies

Mars red as soil
Venus warm as sun, Saturn's glinting rings

Great Bear points Polaris
And I burn envy like the expiring forest

Milky Way tightens
I but a wrinkled pea plant myself hoping

Rains will come
To make this desert a prairie, feed our cattle, our children

Composed on revisiting village (2014)

A Kick in the Throat

"Experience is never at bargain price."
- Alice B. Toklas

No one expects to get cancer. But like the bumper sticker says, "shit happens." November 2017 it happened to me - again.

It began at a friend's dinner party. When I swallowed a piece of meat, my throat began to bleed, slowly seeping up in the back of my mouth. I suggested to Deb quietly that we should leave. The bleeding stopped when we got home, then started again. I spit my way through a messy Saturday night, trying to avoid a trip to the Emergency Room on the weekend. But by Sunday evening, the bleeding wouldn't stop, and I took an ambulance (no siren, thanks) to the hospital.

I spent a night in the ER being poked and prodded, and we stopped the bleeding. I subsequently visited my ENT and was "scoped" which consists of a camera on a flexible tube pushed up your nose and down your throat, giving the ENT a nice video tour of that part of your body. This was the first of several visits to ENTs, and a great number of scopes, eventually leading to a biopsy. The finding: squamous cell cancer on the back center of my tongue. The good news: it's radiation responsive.

After meeting with radiation and surgical oncologists to determine the best way to tackle it, we decided on radiation treatments (37, Monday-Friday for seven weeks) with weekly chemotherapy. It was a regimen effective in 90% of cases. I'd had radiation a few years back for prostate cancer and figured it would be a walk in the park. That's not how it turned out.

I had a port installed in my chest to make chemotherapy administration easy, and since I was healthy, I also had a feeding tube installed in my stomach. The Oncologist suggested that at some point in the treatment, the radiation would make it so hard to eat or drink that nutrition supplement could be administered by the tube. She also told me the tale of a marine that had been a similarly radiation-treated patient. Every morning that guy lined up the necessary bottles of water on his shelf and made himself drink them during the day. The challenge was to get enough liquid and calories into myself daily so as not to have to resort to the feeding tube.

After losing taste and saliva, I developed mouth sores. I went big for protein drinks and calories. I drank 2 liters of liquid a day and made myself eat 2000 calories. As a point of honor I drank and ate enough to not need to use the feeding tube I'd had installed in my stomach. After treatment, the port and tube were removed. I had loved having the port for chemo treatments. I was pleased that I had not needed to use the feeding tube and glad to have it gone.

I decided to go public with my disease and treatment by posting a diary on Facebook, and then posting my status weekly during the chemo treatment. Things went along nicely. Side effects were minimal for a while, then I began to lose my saliva and taste, and symptoms that put you off eating. My public campaign on Facebook documented the journey, the treatments, the pain, the support, and the recovery. Here it is:

Paul's tongue cancer journey on Facebook
November 29, 2017

The Daily Double. Geez.

Test and Prep, Test and Prep
Been testing & prepping for a month or so. Today I had my first chemo (with classic rock & sunshine) & radiation for my new tongue cancer. (Prostate cancer is still under med control.)

I should be alright until about Christmas then feel shitty through January. Great employer, health insurance, & Johns Hopkins health care, Docs/nurses, and a 90% cure rate.

I'll come back to the world in February!

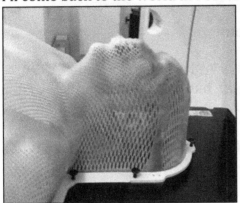

This molded-to-me mask immobilizes me for tumor-targeted radiation. Meditate for 10 minutes. 5 times per week until mid-January.

November 30, 2017
You must visit the dentist before throat radiation, because dentists won't touch your teeth for a while, and you don't wanna get cavities!

December 2, 2017
Thank you everyone for the moving outpouring of support for me in my newest battle with cancer. You move me and I cry with gratitude. But I am a strong Peace Warrior, with great support from family, a top-notch medical team, even prayer warriors, and my global team on my side. We've got this.

Today's radiation music was C, S, N & Y. Tomorrow I'm thinking David Bowie!

December 6, 2017

Week 2: Chemo #2 today. Still cruising! Rock & roll, bit of blues, chin up!

December 13, 2017 - Week Three

Chemo #3 kicking off week 3 treatment. Radiations (10 of 35) are showing their cumulative effects on mouth & throat. Docs say I'm a model patient. I say I'm a Peace Warrior. We've got this.

December 27, 2017 - Week Four

Chemo #4 kicks off wk. 4 of 7. This Friday will be Radiation 18 of 35! Side-effects beginning to ramp up, but I'm still running 5/5 and in control. #RockMusicOverCancer.

Today's radiation soundtrack is Heart, tomorrow ZZ Top, Friday Emerson, Lake & Palmer!!

I'm halfway thru my radiation & chemo treatments! SOOO thankful for my wonderful support team. Debbie my love, and my rock. Also, my family, cousins and friends. I'm getting lots of encouragement & support from all over. I am truly feeling blessed and thankful. Even a Peace Warrior needs a support network. We've got this!

January 3, 2018 - Week Five

Chemo #6 delayed.
Blood test results showed low white blood cell count & Doc changed the plan. Some shots today to boost my whites, Thu & Fri radiation then chemo #6 Monday, inshallah.

No changes in radiation schedule. I'm hooked up anyway just for fluids. Doing fine. We've got this.

January 8, 2018 - Week Six

Bummer blood test results & Doc cancelled chemo #6. Low white blood cell count. It's my body saying "Hey, stop that shit!" Adding some booster shots this wk. & hoping to get it next Monday in wk. 7 (last week) of radiation. Wash hands, avoid crowds, yada yada yada

> Good things that happen when you're getting tongue/neck radiated five days a week and on weekly chemotherapy:
> - You meet the nicest people
> - You don't have to shave anymore
> - You lose a few pounds
> - You get Mark Twain curly hair

January 15 - Week Seven
My little white blood cell factories did their thing!

#LastChemo is flowing, kicking off my last week of radiation treatments! Side-effects hit me this weekend like the famous train - but there's (hyperbole alert) light at the end of this tunnel.

#FeelWorst for next 3 weeks then feel gradually better.

George Harrison "All Things Must Pass" on the headphones and one of my "Shithole country" hats on my head.

January 16, 2018
With apologies to the aptly named Amy Winehouse: They tried to make me go to chemo, & I said no, ah no, ah no!

January 18, 2018
#LastTreatment this morning. Seven weeks X five radiations = 35 sessions bolted to the radiation table by "the mask."

Debbie was there with balloons to celebrate!
January 19
1000-piece jigsaw completed today! (Thanks, Deb, for letting me take half the dining room table.)

January 25 - #WeekZeroPlusOne
A week out. Truckload of bricks hit me two days ago. Been sorting that out since then.

Patience required to feel 10% better per day but the long goal is critical. Yeah, I'm still getting better.

"Look closely to see my tanned throat and curly hair,
My eyes don't change though, and the smile's still there!"

January 29
I'm a Peace Warrior.
I fight cancer!

February 2, 2018 - Week 0 + 2
Now this is recovery! Mucositis (mouth sores) is done, so speech & chewing are much improved. No taste or saliva yet. Neck all crusty. Pain meds doing their thang as the tongue/tumor reconstructs. I'm impatient to get better!

What should I do with my radiation mask? I was snapped to the table 35 times with this device. Smash it? Drive over it? Already considered. Nope. Am leaning toward painting it, so will probably start by cutting it down to "head." Easier to paint and mount the painted head/face, you know? I'm thinking flames blowing back from my nostrils. Ideas welcome!

Week 0 + 3.
The Impatient Patient.
Slow reduction in the actual treatment side-effects of burns, sores, blisters, lost taste, saliva, hair, and hearing, while increasing healing happens & my tongue tumor gradually changes to healthy cells.

February 21, 2018
Stomach tube: OUT
Chest Powerport: OUT

Week 0 + 4
Where I get to torture the mask!
Cut it down & paper-mache.
Paint, buttons & feathers (thanks Nanc).
Me? A bit of taste returns with joy. Hearing loss a new concern.
Doctor visits abound like early spring flowers.

Week 0 + 5
Posted February 22, 2018
The radiation mask becomes art.
"Peace Warrior" represents victory over illness.
The blue-sky background shows health events that float into our lives like falling leaves.
The mask is GB Packer mardi-gras fun, the mouth/throat images the violent cancer site, eyes/tears are pheasant feathers, the lightness continues & shoots out the top in an ultimate celebration of victory.

Special thanks to my sister Nancy for her support, vintage buttons & very special feathers!

Week 0 + 6

Healing is a long-term process. Thank you to the remarkable and far-flung circle of friends and family for your love, support, and prayers. Like some personal health hierarchy, once we've radiated/chemo'd the tongue tumor back into the old testament, and the mouth blisters and skin burns are gone, we have the luxury to become more concerned with lingering treatment side-effects like lymphedema, and newly spotlighted deficiencies in saliva, taste, stamina, and hearing.

The docs say that recovery is a long-term process of addressing what we can with yet a new team of specialists and at the same time discovering (with patience over time) what begins to work again on its own. And it's not an exact science to separate the two categories!

Patience, patients!!

"Dear Valentine" posted March 13, 2018

Week 0 + 8: Finally off the bench & back on the job! Multiple doctors still treating side effects. But I'm coming back!

Sheesh, what a year! It's like the warranty on my body ran out in 2018. It turns out that the tongue cancer was only my <u>first</u> health crisis of 2018. There were three large and several small health crises. And the tongue cancer wasn't even the worst of the three. Here's my summary of the year's health crises.

#1 Tongue Cancer December 2017-March 2018
Emergency room visit, bleeding in throat
Multiple ENT diagnostic visits & video scoping via the nose

Tongue biopsy & Tongue Surgeon consult
Radiation Oncologist selected & treatment program designed
Installed precautionary chemo port & feeding tube
37 targeted radiations (M-F) & 6 chemotherapy sessions
Speech therapy program & daily log to track nutrition and exercise
Multiple hearing tests & fluid removed from inner ear
Lymphedema under chin from radiation & therapy visits
Follow up biopsy
Status: Healed; visit every 3 months, 6 months, *beaucoup* scoping!

#2 Femoral Neuropathy
April-August 2018
Cause: Possibly radiation compromised immune system & treatment-caused inactivity.
Multiple Orthopedists' visits & electromagnetic nerve tests
Epidural steroid injection series for misdiagnosed sciatica
Multiple Neurologists' visits, MRIs: lumbar & neuro
Neurologist and MRI Neuro nailed diagnosis: femoral neuropathy
20 physical therapy sessions to regain use of right leg
Status: Mostly recovered, lost some nerves, no more leg collapses!

#3 Thyroid Conk-out September-October 2018
Likely Cause: Neck Radiation
Rx Oral Medication from my doc
Titration raises doses very gradually; takes forever
Status: Medicating & monitoring via ongoing blood tests

#4 Bladder Radiation Cystitis (This was the bad one)
October 2018 - January 2019
Cause: Prostate cancer radiation - in 2012 can you believe it?
Initial symptoms: Bad hematuria
Emergency Room Admission & 2-week Sibley Hospital stay
3 Operations (clear bladder; Alum Irrigation; Formalin treatment)

#5 Bladder Follow-up Ongoing December 2018 – Present
Surgery (#4) on bladder/urethra connection
Surgery (#5 & #6) on urethral stricture
Hyperbaric Oxygen (HBO) Therapy 40 treatments + 20 (HBOMax)
Status: varying meds, recovering, incontinent

Looking back at the health year-from-hell, I realize how important it is to have a close partner to lean on, to help you stay positive. In so many cases, the disease and the medical or surgical response is your singular focus. It becomes invaluable to have a partner keeping notes during doctor visits, or advocating for you when you're a patient.

The surprise to me is that the after-effects from the various treatments never really leave you. The treatments' side-effects and after-effects can become burdens that you carry forward. They can wear you out or even require further treatments themselves.

I love nurses. Doctors treat the patients, and I certainly appreciate wonderfully skilled doctors. But nurses care for patients. They tell me it's alright to squeeze their hand when the doctor is inserting what amounts to a garden hose through the small opening on the head of my penis. Nurses rescued me repeatedly, even in the long hospital nights when things got clogged and needed the drainage tubes to be "primed" to restart flow. Doctors do the highly skilled interventions. Nurses make healing happen and keep patients sane.

And I love physical therapists. They coached me to regain the use of my legs and to walk again. They measured my progress. When balancing first on one foot for 30 seconds, and then on the other, the therapist pointed out that "Paul, when you started, you couldn't stand on your right leg – at all." Smiles all around.

Thank you, caregivers. I am so fortunate to have had you and my health insurance. Thank you, hospital staff. May I <u>never</u> have another year like that!

But Wait, I'm Not Done!

"Il faut d'abord durer."
- Ernest Hemingway

Looking at me, you'd never know that I'm a stage IV prostate cancer survivor. I turned 67 in May 2019. After some discussion with my boss, we agreed that in July I'd reduce to 80% time. And in December 2019, the month that Debbie turned 65, I officially retired.

Debbie's justifiable fear that I would become a couch potato led me to draft a retirement plan to get her approval. Maybe I did it half to allay her fears, and half to help me see the future. I'd worked pretty much full-time since I was 16. Retirement was always vaguely somewhere in the future. And now it was really happening!

The "plan" is on a single sheet of paper. It's roughly organized by broad categories.

1. First, there's my work. My career of "saving the world" has become personal. I can retire but I can't stop. There will be some engagement with think tanks, guest lecturing, counseling, and mentoring. Maybe a volunteer stint, some paid consulting, and/or board service. My passport was set to expire in May 2021. I checked, and had it renewed.

2. There is some fitness/recreation activity to clearly demonstrate non-couch potato status. Golf occasionally? I can walk with my sweetheart. I can walk the dog, walk in the woods near a river under the guise of fishing (It'll be standing or sitting by a river essentially, with a little walking on each end). General health is a prerequisite.

3. Travel gets its own category. NB: My Retirement Plan was drafted pre-pandemic! When I mention overseas travel to Deb, she usually counters, "Can't we just go back to Paris?" Hard to argue with that. Of course, there are also wonderful places all around Washington DC for an overnight stay. Wine country in Virginia. Maryland's Eastern Shore. Skyline Drive in Virginia. Wine country in Virginia. Harpers Ferry in West Virginia. And of course, there are those wineries in Virginia.

4. Creativity gets space: I can paint and I can write. A couple of years ago I took up acrylic painting. I do it essentially at one "go," lacking the patience and talent to paint with oils. I just sort of zone out, go non-verbal and paint. This makes it an excellent solitary activity – Deb still works Fridays! I'm not talented enough to paint people that you could recognize as humans, but I can do a fair, stylized take on objects that sit still as long as I can. I once took a basic drawing class. And the internet offers a wealth of how-to help. My friends and family are encouraging.

And of course, there are these stories of my life to get down in this memoir. I was dashing pretty headlong looking for adventure remember, not paying attention along the way, with very little notetaking. Putting these notes down has helped me remember the good, the amusing, and sure some trials, but so much adventure – lots of chances to wave at the world.

I have been so riotously fortunate to have flourished in the life categories of both "earth" and "love." I lived all over the wide world and found as my copilot the love of my life. Deb and I explored the world together and I made the world a little better than I found it. We made warm and close friends and laughed way more than average.

Ultimately, Deb and I have together raised two wonderful children to be healthy and kind adults. They are smart and successful. My brother says that in them Debbie and I have recreated ourselves. Jeremy is older, handsome, and has black hair. Nicole, the younger sibling, is beautiful with lighter hair.

And whatever happens in my final years, that's a hell of a finish line for a grand adventure in the world, an adventure that began with a little boy waving at cars on a lonely country road.

CPSIA information can be obtained
at www.ICGtesting.com
Printed in the USA
FSHW012353290821
84382FS